From Social Issues
To Public Policy

Viewpoints On American Politics

EDITOR: SAMUEL KRISLOV

American Legal Processes
WILLIAM MCLAUCHLAN

Congress and the Administrative State
LAWRENCE DODD AND RICHARD SCHOTT

From Social Issues to Public Policy
ROBERT EYESTONE

Mass Media and Politics
NORMAN LUTTBEG

From Social Issues To Public Policy

Robert Eyestone
University of Minnesota

JOHN WILEY & SONS
New York   Chichester   Brisbane   Toronto

Library of Congress Cataloging in Publication Data:

Eyestone, Robert, 1942-
From social issues to public policy.

(Viewpoints on American politics)
Includes index.
1. United States—Politics and government.
2. United States—Social policy.   3. Political
participation—United States.   4. Policy sciences.
5.   Public administration—Decision making.   I.   Title.
JK271.E97   309.1′73′092   78–13334
ISBN 0-471-24978-5

Printed in the United States of America

10 9 8 7 6 5 4 3

Preface

The overriding question in this book is one of process: how are social issues resolved and translated into public policies? One obvious complication is that some issues are not translated into public policy at all. But this too is a matter of process—why are some issues responded to but not resolved? Why, and how, are some issues denied a hearing in the halls of government, and what are the consequences of nonresponse?

Governmental responsiveness and the cost of government are perennially at odds in a democratic society. Citizens, in exercising their prerogatives as stingy taxpayers, are likely to starve the governmental bodies supposedly working for the public's benefit. Politicians, in corresponding fashion, are often tempted to promise the impossible. They try to respond to social demands with inadequate resources, and often with only the most tenuous public commitment to the solution of social problems. Often the result of this tension between politicians and voters is public unhappiness, cynicism, or fatalism. In this book I attempt to explain why this state of affairs is found so frequently in American politics. I hope that the book may help readers develop realistic expectations for government action, and that it may improve the chances of getting effective policy responses for those issues where governmental action can be beneficial.

The organizational plan of the book is straightforward. First is the matter of definition. What are social issues? What are the political features that may be important in understanding how they are translated into public policy? There follows next (Chapters 2 and 3) an approach to the problems of politicians and government bureaucrats. When is it reasonable to expect government response? What can governments do, and what kinds of problems might they be well advised to stay away from?

Chapters 4 and 5 present a model of how social issues should, or could, be translated into public policy if everything works just right. This view of the overall response process makes it easier to isolate defects and weak spots in the process when response failures occur, as they inevitably will. Chapters 6 and 7 then attempt to identify the reasons for various kinds of nonresponse and to distinguish unsatisfactory responses from complete response failures.

Chapter 8 examines the impact of the broad sweep of political events on governmental response to social issues. What happens in a crisis? What do noncrisis responses look like? How are responses routinized?

The final chapter reviews the argument of the book and offers advice for improving the quality of political responses to social issues. How can the limited capacities of governments be expanded or supplemented? How can claims be advanced in more compelling fashion? What private resources are necessary to ensure satisfactory public response? How can they be applied most effectively?

I acknowledge happily Sam Krislov's comments on the first draft of the book, the many useful suggestions on the second draft my Jeffrey Miller and Michael Smith, and Wayne Anderson's editorial patience. As in the past, the hand of my wife, Susan, can be seen in the niceties of the punctuation.

Robert Eyestone

Contents

1

Politics and the Universe of Issues

What Is an Issue?

Issues are the fuel of politics, sustaining the fires of conflict and controversy; or when tamed and transmuted to bureaucratic responses, providing the energy for the day-to-day business of government. The customary image of political issues is that of transitory events or controversies arising rapidly, reaching a peak of public interest and involvement, and subsiding again. In this process an issue may become clearer or more murky; it may be redefined several times as different groups participate in the debate and different points of view are expressed; it may be denied, neglected, ignored, spurned, shunted aside or moderated by politicians and governmental officials; and it may be resolved, responded to in part, or simply displaced in public interest when something more compelling comes along.

Politics deals in the transitory. The public's memory for broken promises and unanswered questions is usually short (a blessing for politicians) but so is its memory for personalities and achievements ("but what have you done for me lately?"). In contrast, social issues are much more likely to reflect the enduring questions of the social order: what is happening to the family? what has become of the traditional moral values? what can be done to improve racial harmony? how can crime and violence be reduced? Social concerns such as these are truly enduring: they

1

seem to move in a time scale outside the bounds of politics, and in many instances they are not clear-cut issues so much as puzzling questions to which there are many answers and no single satisfactory response.

Only infrequently can these two divergent perspectives be brought together, for they do indeed represent different worlds of ideas and actions. Although this book emphasizes the immediately political side of public issues—those events, groups, and institutions close to the making of public policy decisions—it also seeks to identify and describe the circumstances in which social issues break loose from the shapeless mass of social musings, become clearer in outline, become identified as problems for which governmental action might be a possible solution, and finally enter the political process as explicit demands or proposals for public policy.

This issue translation process is not a simple or easy one. More than chance is required to bring most issues from their obscure origins into active consideration on decision-making agendas. The self-interested motivations of lobbyists, bureaucrats, elected politicians, and other political entrepreneurs must be engaged to stoke the political fires, and it is in this complex process that the clues to governmental responsiveness, or lack of it, must be sought. Issues *are* the fuel of politics because they attract the attention and mobilize the energies of large numbers of people who are not ordinarily involved in political life, and because professional politicians and bureaucrats are compelled to come to terms with this outpouring of political energy. It is *their* reaction that clarifies choices or obscures them, and that advances an issue toward a constructive resolution or shunts it aside.

Some Definitions

In common usage, the term "issue" means a number of things. Often it is synonymous with "problem," "question," "controversy," or even "scandal." In all these instances it is a word that calls for action: it carries the connotation of a matter requiring immediate public attention. Thus the Watergate affair, the

Russian wheat deal, the pornography crisis, the unemployment problem, the drug epidemic, the amnesty question, the budget controversy, the conflict over school busing, the abortion issue, and many similar public questions have at one time or another been referred to as issues. Some of these are ephemeral, arising from the actions of particular politicians; others are nonrecurring, with action choices already made before the general public is aware of the need to decide. Many so-called issues are worked up for election campaigns, and discarded at inauguration day. What was the lasting significance of the missile gap, the Bobby Baker case, or the Pueblo incident? What purpose is served by continuing discussion of radical conspiracies, presidential pardons, or the private morality of national political leaders?

Other political questions, perhaps just as fleeting in their claim on public attention, are offshoots of more enduring social concerns. They come into the public eye momentarily because they have reached some critical point of development, because some decisive action is about to be taken or some irrevocable decision made, because a high level of conflict is involved, or because their effects are particularly severe or fall heavily on some large identifiable group of people. Pornography and forceful protest, for example, have influenced the development of constitutional free speech guarantees even though they are no longer important as national issues. The 1973 energy crisis encouraged international cooperation on energy policy and domestic questioning of energy-wasteful life styles.

It will be useful to distinguish among issues, controversies, conflicts, questions, and concerns to highlight those features of issues that account for their rough or smooth passage through the American political process. An issue is a special kind of political situation, with identifiable causes or sources, definite characteristics, and a limited number of possible outcomes. The remainder of this chapter considers the sources of issues.

An issue arises when a public with a problem seeks or demands governmental action, and there is public disagreement over the best solution to the problem.

A public: How many people make a public? Certainly it is not necessary to involve every citizen or even every citizen of voting age, to have an issue. Some while ago E.E. Schattschneider suggested that 60 million people, or about 60% of the adult population of the time, constituted the politically active segment.[1] Roger W. Cobb and Charles D. Elder suggest a figure of 10% for the attentive public,[2] the fraction of the total population that follows and understands current events. But demands for governmental action come from groups much smaller than either of these, and they are listened to favorably. Functional groups, especially, may gain sympathetic treatment out of apparent proportion to their numbers because they can, if they act in concert, disrupt social and economic processes affecting far larger numbers of people. If all the doctors (or even a large fraction of them), all the truck drivers, all the computer operators, or all the fire fighters in a community stopped working, their complaints would be listened to much more quickly than the complaints of a random sample of the public of similar size. So the definition of a "public" is bound to be somewhat slippery. It presumably must take account of the important fact of political life that organization, or a critical social or economic position, may be equivalent in political effect to a much larger size in sheer numbers. In addition, the interests of some groups in a particular issue may seem legitimate while the interests of other groups may not seem so. Perhaps we could say that a public is any group that is important enough that we feel it *should* be listened to, at least on some issues. It is then a matter for observation whether a group that can generate an issue in one subject area is big or important enough to generate an issue in any other area it chooses.

Practically speaking, most politically important groups *are* small in size. Politicians do not expect highly articulate mass uprisings; instead, they try to estimate the extent of silent support for a position from the intensity of its advocates and the expansiveness of their claims. These matters are discussed in

[1] E. E. Schattschneider, *The Semisovereign People,* New York, Holt, Rinehart and Winston, 1960, pp. 106–7.

[2] Roger W. Cobb and Charles D. Elder, *Participation in American Politics: The Dynamics of Agenda Building,* Boston, Allyn and Bacon, 1972, pp. 104–11.

more detail in connection with the setting of the public agenda, Chapter 4.

With a problem: A problem is simply some state of affairs that annoys, hinders, or injures the complaining group. Since it is their prerogative to complain about anything that displeases them, there is no way to delimit a class of acceptable problems around which issues may be generated. For the definition, any problem is as good as any other. It most certainly is not true, however, that just any old problem will gain a sympathetic response from governmental officials, or from members of the general public not directly affected by it. Some claimed problems will be regarded as "natural disasters," normal business risks, unfortunate but uncontrollable results of economic processes; unhappy but perfectly natural consequences of social hierarchy, and so on. The low status and small financial compensation traditionally accorded teachers have not been regarded as social injustice by anyone other than teachers. The high cost of medical malpractice insurance gained little public attention until groups of doctors began withholding their services in protest.

The identification of an acceptable problem is not entirely a matter of sympathy among social classes, or of mass sympathy for the pleadings of special interests. Where a responding governmental institution is dominated by groups with particular biases, it may display this bias by differential response to different problems expressed by the same group of clients. The legitimacy of some complaints may be denied because the solutions to them would be too costly, too difficult, or would go against the interests of the classes or groups dominating the government. For instance, city governments dominated by downtown business interests, or rural-dominated state legislatures, will not be very sympathetic to the unemployment problems of urban ghetto residents.

So again there is substantial ambiguity in identifying a problem appropriate to our definition of a social issue, just as it is hard to decide how big a public might be. Nevertheless, some judgment on the matter of valid complaints underlies any attempt to evaluate the responsiveness of a particular set of political institutions. This point will be taken up again in later chapters.

Demands government action: It is not always easy to tell when a group is demanding governmental action. Not every social issue is presented publicly, and not every public issue is phrased in terms of governmental action. Some issues relate to the distribution of valuables through institutions other than government, even though their resolution may be conditioned by governmental policies and actions; in others the claimants do not expect to gain immediate recognition of their views, but work instead toward a gradual public awareness of the issue.

Beyond this, a group formed of nonpoliticians, a group of politically inexperienced people, or a group bringing a problem to government officials for the first time may not know exactly what it wants. To be sure, it wants an effective response to its problem, but it may not know what sorts of responses are possible and it may not know, strategically, what would be best to ask for. A group approaching the government with only a vague "fix it, please" may more readily be dismissed or bought off cheaply than a group that is experienced, knows the key officials to petition, and knows the right time to make a request. But groups that already know these things are also the most adept at getting what they want without precipitating an issue. Theirs are inside strategies, designed specifically to keep the group's profile as low as possible to avoid potential opposition groups waiting for an appeal through other channels.

A demand for governmental remedies is not necessarily the first choice of a group seeking to solve a problem, since as a strategy it may be costly, of uncertain value, and potentially risky. The group may even lose other benefits it currently enjoys if its pleas are exposed to scrutiny in the public arena. Real estate developers seeking a special tax credit would not begin with a public information campaign showing the inequities of current tax laws. Such an approach would almost surely backfire, and it would, in any case, invite other claimants to parade *their* favorite charities before the public. Developers may be forced to *defend* their tax breaks if the conflict does become public, but their first approach certainly should be directed to the legislative tax writing committees and to friendly home state senators.

Relatively few concrete actions indicate that an appeal for governmental intervention is being made. Such actions might include direct petitions to executive agencies, legislative proposals introduced by friendly legislators, lobbying on existing legislative proposals, and attempts to lobby for specific proposals in party and candidate platforms. Other possibilities, such as public opinion campaigns, contributions to reelection campaigns, and endorsement of candidates, may be indirect attempts to influence governmental actions, but they are generally designed to supplement more direct methods. Mass media advertising creates a favorable climate within which direct requests might be acted upon, and campaign involvement is a way of buying access to the winning side when it gets into office.

If for some reason our definition was asked to identify every social question as either a social issue or not, solely on the basis of the "demand for governmental action" criterion, its application would necessarily be arbitrary and frustrating. Social questions sometimes become issues, issues sometimes lose their issue status before they are resolved, and the parties to a social conflict may even disagree among themselves about whether their differences are truly social issues. Indeed, it would be surprising if social questions did *not* change over time in the way they are presented, in the nature of the political coalitions concerned with them, and in the kinds of remedies being sought by the various parties to the conflict.

Labor-management relations provide a good illustration of these definitional problems. Usually they proceed peacefully within the framework provided by the National Labor Relations Act (the Wagner Act and Taft-Hartley), or a similar state law. Grievances, strikes, and contract agreements are handled without questioning this public policy framework and without precipitating a public dispute. Presidential powers may be invoked in certain disputes such as national coal, railroad, or steel strikes, under the terms of the Taft-Hartley Act or the Railway Labor Act. These emergency powers represent a limited solution to the issue of excessive or irresponsible union power, but their discretionary application (or a failure to use them) may become a matter of public controversy in any specific strike, even though the abstract need for them has been accepted.

In a few instances, labor-management clashes have generated new public issues even when they began as wholly private disputes or as private disputes under neutral government regulation. In their initial organizing efforts in the California grape industry, the United Farm Workers under Cesar Chavez relied on traditional labor organizing techniques. Many table and wine grape growers signed agreements with the UFW in the 1960s. Gallo, however, had signed a contract with the Teamsters and was subjected to continued demonstrations and sporadic boycotts organized by Chavez. For a long time the UFW relied on a private strategy of economic pressure, with some public support through a selective boycott, but with no direct appeal to government. Gallo's response was to declare support for extending NLRA coverage to migrant workers, and to attempt to rouse public opinion to this position through such devices as an "open letter" published in newspapers throughout the country, urging readers to write their representatives to extend legislative protection to farm workers.

Happily there is no need to say that one side or the other in the grape dispute is correct in its identification of the issue, but it is important that at least one of the parties regards the question as a public matter requiring a legislative solution. It is this belief that raises the dispute to a potential public issue, whether both sides feel that way or not, and whether there is much likelihood of governmental response or not.

Disagreement about solutions: If there is a key element in the definition of an issue, it is that of disagreement about proposed solutions. The fact of disagreement can usually be seen plainly when an issue is under active discussion. Nevertheless, disagreement is not synonymous with overt controversy or conflict. The opposing sides of an issue need not always confront each other directly, and disagreement need not always be acrimonious, violent, or disruptive. The image of a typical public issue *does* involve confrontation and vigorous and heated debate, but these extremes are not always found in practice. Intelligent adversaries seek influence wherever they can rather than trying to defeat their opponents on their opponents' chosen ground; thus while an issue may be "joined," it may be joined only obliquely, with the two sides working through different points of access to the political process. For instance, labor spokesmen usually find allies in the Labor Department or among Democrats in Congress, and their business opponents often work through the Commerce Department or through individual friendly legislators. The pluralistic nature of the American policy process often mutes direct conflict, but differences of opinion must still be accommodated in the ultimate resolution of a social issue.

When Is an Issue an Issue?

A basic thesis regarding demands made in the public arena is that the style of politics and the resulting distribution of rewards are fundamentally different from those found in the absence of public discussion. Democratic theorists go a step further to say that the consequences of open decisions are always preferable to any kind of closed politics. For them, it is a perverse reflection on the genius of American politics that we have managed to create, within such a seemingly open political system, so many hidden niches where favor-seekers can meet with favor-providers face-to-face and undisturbed by critics or opponents.

In one very important sense, however, the privatized political sector and the open, public, combative, issue-dominated political sector are simply two stages of the same process. An issue goes through several steps, beginning with its initial appearance on the public agenda, moving through a period of maximum controversy, then (usually) reaching some kind of temporary resolution. If the issue is resolved, even temporarily, by the creation of a specific governmental device—a study group, an agency, a program, a new legal category or status—then there will usually be some enduring carryover regardless of the issue's subsequent course. When interest groups enjoy open and easy access to governmental channels, the receptivity of those channels can usually be traced to an earlier policy decision which was intended as a resolution of some issue, even if it was expected at the time to have only a limited or temporary life. Most such responses outlive the issues that generated them, thus governments at all levels accumulate these institutionalized monuments to what may originally have been expedient responses to short-term political problems.

The Resettlement Administration provides an interesting, if minor, illustration of the tenacity of government programs. Created by executive order in 1935 to administer large-scale resettlement programs in response to the problem of Dust Bowl emigrants, it was transferred to the Department of Agriculture by executive order at the end of 1936, and it became the Farm Security Administration in 1937. Legislative action in 1946 abolished the FSA, but many of its programs were taken over by the newly created Farmers Home Administration. The FmHA still exists, administering loan programs dating back to the Bankhead-Jones Farm Tenant Act of 1937, as well as newer ones created by the 1964 Economic Opportunity Act.

Nothing in politics is ever entirely new. Every issue has been seen before, in some form or other; consequently for most kinds of issues there is a favored point of access to the government. As a result, the joining of an issue may be an instance of delayed reaction—a counterdemand may not emerge until the initial claimant group has taken its request to what it considers to be the appropriate governmental agency. The appearance of this demand may then produce an issue, as potential opponents sense that their interests are at stake if they do not themselves participate in the decisions about to be made.

A potential issue will not be joined unless the opposition to the initial claimants thinks that it has something to gain, or a loss to prevent, by becoming involved. Thus an issue always implies a gain *and* a loss—a zero sum situation—but it implies something more. To appear as an issue, a social policy question must pose a substantial threat of loss to at least one of the concerned parties, and for a potential issue to become an issue in reality, the two opposing sides must associate this threat with a governmental response favorable to the other side.

For these reasons, the early stages in the life of any policy—when it is still a matter of controversy and debate—are most relevant to the study of social issues. A few issues are generated by opposition to, criticism of, or the breakdown of existing governmental programs, but most make their appearance as unresolvable social or economic problems that go beyond any established policy. Although this book does not treat institutionalized responses to social issues in great detail, it is important to remember that the responses to most conflicts over issues create enduring structures, and these in turn color routine governmental response to the numerous social and economic concerns that never reach the high levels of controversy or mass involvement characteristic of social issues. For instance, the proponents of an independent Consumer Protection Agency were certainly aware that the immediate consequences of such a plan would be largely symbolic because it would take the agency some time to staff itself, collect and coordinate the programs transferred to it from other agencies, and so on. Instead of hoping for an immediate impact while consumerism issues were still politically potent, they were looking forward to establishing regular lines of access for consumer viewpoints similar to those already enjoyed by big and small business, labor, agriculture, and other organized and traditionally powerful groups. The availability of routinized responses does not rule out the possibility of radical changes in public policy, but it may prejudice the chances of success for radical demands by providing an easy "out" for politicians confronted with such demands. This point is taken up again in Chapter 8.

Why Is the Definition so Complicated?

It must be tempting to say, "We all know what public issues are—let's get on with the business at hand." There probably is substantial agreement on the identity of the major social issues in the United States in the past few decades, and in that intuitive sense we all *do* know what public issues are. But the purpose of this elaborate definition is to point out politically significant aspects of social issues more than to foster agreement on a canon of certified issues. The emerging picture shows a dismaying variety of opportunities for failure of political response. An issue is associated with one or more publics, but these may be too small or politically unimportant to command attention. An issue embodies a distinct problem, but it may be only a minor concern to society at large, or a matter on which most politicians have already formed their opinions. Government action is demanded, but the demand may be made in the wrong place or to the wrong people, or it may call for a response beyond governmental capabilities. Finally, there is disagreement, and this in itself provides all the excuse for inaction a determined politician would ever need. With all these handicaps, social issues can hardly be expected to resolve themselves. The last section of this chapter considers whether the appeal to government is inevitable, and the next chapter then looks at the political circumstances that seem most conducive to issue resolution.

Are Issues Inherently Political?

Here is a selected list of policy questions that have concerned Congress over the past few years. All private bills have been excluded, all routine appropriations and tax measures, all internal reforms, and all items of less than national importance, although many questions on the list may still have strongly differential effects on geographic regions and social and economic classes.

truth in lending
national redwoods park
cigarette advertising ban
mine safety
funding for the SST
rail passenger services
loan guarantees for Lockheed
enforcement of equal employment opportunity
trans-Alaska oil pipeline
Consumer Protection Agency

no-fault auto insurance
school busing
school prayers
campaign spending reform
strip mining regulation
emergency public jobs
wage and price controls
sugar shortages
oil embargo
sex discrimination
natural gas price deregulation
abortion
federal housing programs
occupational safety and health standards
handgun control
food stamps
foreign bribery by corporations
riot control
draft reform
the Carswell and Haynsworth nominations to the Supreme
    Court
approval for the ABM
organized crime
postal reform
Vietnam troop withdrawal
18-year-old vote
Indian claims
presidential war powers limitation
termination of Cambodia bombing
no-knock police entry
capital punishment
Nixon impeachment
Nixon pardon
tax cuts and spending ceilings
tax reform
guidelines for intelligence operations
New York City bankruptcy
amnesty for draft evaders

This may not be a complete list of all social issues of the early 1970s, because some may not have been expressed as legislative proposals, but it does seem to capture a great many of the significant questions of the period.

One use to which such a list can be put is an assessment of how necessary governmental action is to the resolution of social issues. Logically speaking, governmental action is not the only response to a social issue, nor is it the only response that will be satisfying to the mass public or to those members of the public who are most directly concerned with the issue. Narrowly defined, social issues focus on social or economic problems regardless of the extent of current government involvement in those problems. Despite our tendency to appeal to government when anything goes wrong, political involvement is neither inevitable nor always preferable. Other institutions in the society such as organized religion, private charity, schools, the medical and legal professions, the family, and even the economic market are often the best locus of response for certain kinds of social issues, though governmental authority may be kept in reserve as a last resort when a signal failing occurs in one of these non-governmental alternatives.

Of the 47 items on the list of recent issues, the first 27, or 57% of the total, occurred in policy areas where the role of government itself is at issue. In fact, the federal government *has* been involved in each of the 27 in some way or other, but in each instance governmental action has taken the form of intervention in social or economic processes that would continue even if all governmental involvement ceased. Specific issues in each of these areas would be resolved "naturally" without further government intervention, although it is unlikely that we would be happy with the results in every case. Logging companies would decide for themselves how many redwoods should be saved and how many clear-cut, the supersonic transport either would or would not attract private financial backing, local communities would decide for themselves whether to have prayers in school or not, the labor market would determine how many workers were unemployed, sugar prices would adjust to the level of sugar production, handgun sales would proceed without regulation, and so on.

The remaining 20 items on the list are inherently political in the sense that they revolve around specific politicians, certain undisputed functions of government such as maintenance of public order and national security, the rights of citizens with respect to the government, or methods for financing governmental operations. The exact numbers of "inherently political issues" and "issues of governmental role" are not critical, but it is probably significant that these two types appear with roughly equal frequency. Changes in society, in the political party in power, and in the world situation may lead politicians to be more inward-looking or more outward-looking from one year to the next, but in the long run some balance probably prevails.

Controversies about government personnel are in some ways the most obvious political issues. The Supreme Court must be staffed; the residents of every congressional district have a right to one representative in Congress; the Presidency must be filled somehow, even if the choices are not very appealing. The so-called issues of most election campaigns are strongly personal as well: Would you buy a used car from this man? Is he presidential timber? Is candidate X trigger-happy? Is candidate Y inclined to flip-flop? These personal qualities of the candidates are as important as the vague comments they make on specific policy questions (what used to be called "campaign promises").

Scandals involving political figures are ambiguous instances of inherently political issues. The remedy is clear enough—"throw the rascals out"—but the cause, and therefore the ultimate remedy, often remains as a worrisome question. One symptom is difficulty in identifying precise, resolvable issues implicit in political scandal. Consider the Watergate affair. Without question, Watergate fell into the inherently political category. The honesty of Richard Nixon and his governmental and political associates was at issue. But what was "the issue"—what was the policy question that cried out for an answer?

One issue that did crystallize under the influence of the Watergate catalyst might be stated this way: "how can campaign financing be reformed so that the undue influence of corporations and the rich is minimized?" Congress, in seeking to resolve this issue, appears to have seen the problem as one of "cleaning their own house," and the reform measures introduced by the

1974 campaign finance act were therefore applied to congressional as well as presidential campaign financing. The financial disclosure rules and external income limitations the House and Senate imposed on themselves in 1977 are additional evidence of congressional reaction along these lines.

Another Watergate issue that was much discussed but never resolved was, "can we do anything more to ensure the honesty of our political leaders?" This is a perennial issue, of course, reflecting a deep-seated American distrust of people who make their living from government. Americans expect their government to reflect the best in American society and to correct the worst; when it reflects less than the best no one can be sure where the fault lies. By their nature, these issues probably cannot be resolved. Their solution must come from forces outside politics because the basic honesty or dishonesty of politicians—at least those at the highest levels of national office—is probably fixed by the time they are recruited for high office. The problem is unsolvable because no one could argue seriously that the family, schools, or religion can do more to produce honest candidates for public office than they do now. All those people involved in Watergate were products of families and schools, and most were influenced in some way by religious teachings, but the moral precepts of these social institutions do not seem to have survived the rigors of Washington. Nor can this kind of solution be imagined to operate retroactively—another "dose" of honesty cannot be administered effectively to a free adult whose basic moral values and patterns of behavior have been set for some time.

Another insurmountable difficulty in attempting to fall back on nonpolitical institutions for the solution to political issues is that such issues often contain an element of crisis that demands a quick response. Although the influence of nonpolitical institutions may be profound and pervasive, it is unlikely to change level or direction very rapidly because these institutions are essentially "headless." There simply is no effective way to ask private charities to give more attention to social issues, or to ask families to work harder at inculcating moral values, or to direct the market to distribute goods and services in some manner radically different from that currently employed. Change could occur only if these institutions were displaced by governmental mechanisms or brought under substantial governmental control.

Alternate Issue Definitions

A neat distinction between political and nonpolitical issues often cannot be maintained. The greatest complication is that government and other, nonpolitical, institutions are related in ways that are mutually limiting. The blame for any emerging social difficulty may therefore be thrown to government or to some social institution, or to both. When a problem emerges in an area already "covered" by government activity, the issue may be defined as the result of a policy failure and a resolution may be sought in a change of policy. Alternately, it is possible to define the issue to avoid government action—the problem may be required to solve itself, it may be declared to be a nonproblem, or it may be declared unsolvable under current circumstances.

As an example, consider the problem of teenage unemployment. Since the federal government is committed, in the Employment Act of 1946, to maintain high levels of employment and to attempt to find or stimulate job opportunities for everyone willing to work, the phenomenon of teenage unemployment might be seen as a failure of existing policy. If this view is taken, the issue is "can the government do something *more* to provide jobs for teenagers?"

One element of existing policy identified as a possible contributor to teenage unemployment is federal minimum wage legislation. The argument here is that the nature of teenage job openings—usually summer jobs, part-time or temporary positions—is such that they should not fall under minimum wage coverage. On the whole, teenage job holders are likely to be less experienced and less valuable to an employer than a seasoned worker put in the same position; therefore employers should be allowed to hire teenagers at wages below those set by minimum wage laws. Further, teenagers seeking jobs are usually not supporting a family, or even fully supporting themselves, and therefore the notion of holding wage levels high enough to provide a "living wage" is inappropriate for teenagers and may diminish the number of jobs being offered to them.

An alternate view of teenage unemployment stresses many of the same things, in particular the presumption that teenagers are not in the labor force from economic necessity, but it comes to a different conclusion. By redefining the real social problem of unemployment as that of unemployed family heads, some economists and politicians—including President Nixon and his Secretary of the Treasury John Connally—attempted to dismiss teenage unemployment as a nonproblem. They argued that unemployment for this category of worker was not serious for family income stability, that it would inevitably be much higher than unemployment rates for family heads, and that the only appropriate response would be to seek statistical "full employment" for the aggregate labor force. In brief, this approach denied that there was, or should be, anything special about teenage unemployment levels. For those directly affected, the official point of view was that the problem would have to solve itself.

We can see, then, considerable ambiguity in the idea that every social issue requires a governmental response. The issues that are unquestionably governmental are often fleeting in nature, and there is the nagging sense that the root cause of some is actually social and not governmental after all. For those issues where governmental involvement is itself controversial, the relative impact of existing governmental policy and other social institutions is hard to untangle and it is therefore hard to determine how much improvement could be expected from a change in policy. Nevertheless, the distinction is useful because it highlights the initial public reaction to these two issue categories, and it indicates an important difference in the nature of public expectations about issue resolution. For governmental issues the initiative is expected to be internal; for other issues the question of the proper role for government must first be decided, and some of the initiative in resolving these issues is forced back onto issue publics themselves. Some form of governmental response may eventually emerge in both cases, but the processes will be quite different.

2

What to Expect from Politics

It is common these days to hope that governments will deal with almost every kind of social and economic ill; it is equally common to criticize the public for an unreflective belief in the capacities of government. In fact, the American public displays cycles of buoyant faith and sharp disillusionment with government power, and the long-term trend shows a gradual erosion in the credibility of political promises.[1] But governments are still the ultimate forum within which to raise issues and seek their solution. Instead of turning our backs on politics, the point is to know what we can and cannot expect from government.

These next chapters consider the general circumstances surrounding government response to social issues. We examine first the suitability of a social issue for governmental response, as seen by the general public and by politicians. Issue translation occurs within a context of elite and mass attitudes, and it is important to see how this "public politics" affects the likelihood of response.

Second, from the governmental viewpoint we look at three major limitations on government action and establish some requisites for governmental response to social issues. Governments must correctly identify a social problem or issue, they must have the capacity to respond, and politicians must be persuaded that

---

[1] John E. Mueller, "Presidential Popularity from Truman to Johnson," *American Political Science Review*, **LXIV** (1970), pp. 18–34.

they should respond, before there is much chance of effective governmental response to a social issue. Lacking a clear definition of the issue, government action risks being gratuitous—"we're doing this for your own good." Lacking the capacity for action, governments risk being overambitious—"the need was so pressing, we just had to do something." Acting without a strong political rationale may be whimsical—"it seemed like a good idea at the time."

These two approaches are complementary; together they should provide a broad understanding of the issue response process, as a prelude to the study of specific issues.

The Nature of Political Responses

We hope that social issues brought into the political arena will be resolved with reasonable dispatch, and that such issues will then be removed from the public's list of problems. To distinguish real resolution from a variety of other outcomes, let us say that a resolution is a positive action by governmental policymakers that is sufficiently satisfying to the major sides of the conflict that they do not immediately raise the issue, or a related issue, again.

Actually, resolution is just one member of a broader category of attempted resolutions, in which governmental policymakers try to satisfy claimants through positive actions of some kind, but fail. Their actions may please no one, they may please some but not all, or they may divert claims by redirecting them against government policy responses themselves. Within this broader category, strict conditions are placed on "resolutions" so that they can be identified unequivocally without reference to the attitudes of former claimants, but merely by looking at their actions.

By the nature of issues and politics, unsuccessful attempted resolutions are likely to be more numerous than successful ones. Honest government responses may produce failures—nonresolutions—of different types, of which the most important may be called diverted issues, deferred issues, and displaced issues. Diverted issues are simply those that are redefined by their advocates because governmental response to the initial definition was unsatisfactory. Deferred issues are "pure" cases of failure, where governmental efforts are seen by most or all concerned groups to be immediately unacceptable (without waiting for further information on the policy's effects), and where the same issue is brought up at the next opportunity. Displaced issues are those in which the focus of controversy shifts from the original issue to the policy response, or to another issue entirely.

A narrow line distinguishes these three types of failure from temporarily resolved issues, but the distinction is crucial for theorizing about and evaluating the issue translation process. The distinction resolves around the nature of reasonable expectations and the centrality of the time dimension in policy processes. Put in briefest form, the argument is this: It is reasonable to expect an honest government response if an issue is pushed hard enough and long enough, but it is not reasonable to expect a guarantee of success. Further, it is usually unreasonable to expect an *immediate* response—issues that have been deferred have not been denied, nor have they been resolved. They can and usually will recur, and if the original claimants pursue the issue, they will find that the chances of a satisfactory resolution have not necessarily been lowered as a result of waiting.

In any short time interval, a large number of American political issues may appear to be ignored. Over a period of several months, for instance, no governmental official or elected politician may make any statement or appear to express any concern about welfare reform. Does this mean that the poverty issue is being ignored? Strictly speaking it probably does mean that, but a lack of response in the short term may be unreliable evidence about the ultimate responsiveness of the American political process. Claimants are always impatient to see some action. To maintain internal group interest and momentum, and to put group resources to most efficient use, interest group leaders hope for responses that politicians would likely regard as unduly hasty. Movement of any kind is useful in the never-ending task of mobilizing the faithful; politicians prefer to delay and be sure of their ground before committing themselves or public resources.

Another confounding characteristic of American political life at every level is the coincidence of public issues. When more than one significant issue is being discussed in the mass media and worried about by average citizens, some may temporarily be pushed aside as the focus of debate shifts from one to another. Also, for a number of reasons (publicity, simplicity, personal preferences, lack of resources, political pressures) politicians often prefer to deal with one problem at a time. While running around putting out fires (or adding fuel to them) they will often appear to be ignoring those issues that they have assigned lower priority. Further, there is no reason to assume that politicians will have the same priorities as the general public. Since there are always enough problems for politicians to deal with, they may actually ignore some issues regarded as serious by the public because they are busy responding to other issues on whose seriousness they and the public are in agreement. An issue invested with more seriousness by the public than by governmental officials may have to persist longer, or build up a bigger head of steam, before it can claim a response.

Issues that emerge suddenly (like fires) and seem susceptible to easy solutions (like putting out fires rather than preventing them) will get higher priority than the persistent issues for which nobody has yet thought up a satisfactory response. Racially segregated housing patterns persist in most cities, and become more segregated year after year, while "neat" issues like public funding for domed sports arenas come up and are dispatched with relative ease.

Some kinds of response failures are more serious than others. Diverted issues are not matters for serious concern because the original claimants will return, in time, with a modified list of demands. Deferred issues will also be raised again, and will become instances of unsatisfactory response only if there seems to be little possibility of changes in the political conditions under which the issues were first deferred. Displaced issues may or may not be unproductive diversions. If the energies of the original claimant groups are taken up and exhausted in debates over government policies, the original social issue may just as well have been denied. Even if claimants return to the displaced substantive issue once the secondary conflict over government policy has been resolved, they are likely to be no further along the road to achieving a satisfactory resolution of the initial issue. If they *have* made any progress, it is only to have identified some government policies as unworkable.

This pattern is common in the welfare area. The intractability of income maintenance problems, and the inherent conflicts among design criteria for income transfer programs, make critics in the welfare field only too willing to drop the issue itself and to take up sides on each new proposal as it comes along. When a new proposal—the Job Corps, for instance, or children's allowances, or the Family Assistance Plan—has been tried or analyzed and found unsatisfactory, everyone returns to the original issue. Unfortunately, the debate about welfare is little better informed for this excursion into the specifics of one particular income transfer scheme.

Although issues are often displaced, displacement cannot be a sensible government policy in most instances because it poses greater dangers for politicians than the available alternatives. An issue can only be displaced by another, for which the same response expectations may apply. This explains why economic problems, for example, are such a political liability. A president must have an economic policy, even if it is not thought out, because there is no way to avoid the use of the economic policy mechanisms of spending and taxation. Thus the president always faces the risk of being criticized for making the wrong choice when his "policy" ultimately fails.

Any discussion of claimant groups and satisfaction of their demands must include the possibility that their positions have been substantially altered by group leaders for reasons of strategy. Issue publics do not necessarily "know" what they want to do when their original positions meet with rebuff. Indeed, their original positions were also themselves modified to some degree by guidance they received from group leaders, who in turn based their recommendations on the probabilities that certain kinds of changes could be achieved. Group leaders, with a perpetual need to "produce" for their constituents, may recommend strategies that further the displacement of social by governmental issues. To the extent that these recommendations are self-serving foremost, and only secondarily designed to serve the interests of their clients, they may contribute to a real problem of response failure.

Here again it is difficult to evaluate the seriousness of these distortions because they assume the objective reality of the "real interests" of mass publics. Unfortunately, large groups do not articulate clear issue positions. Further, aggregation of the positions taken by individuals, even if they are in fact clearly expressed, will not always produce a clear group position—because of the inevitable variation in intensity and direction of individual opinions it will usually *not* do so. The "real interests" of any group must, necessarily, be speculative as well, but the intent of this book is to catalogue and discuss gaps in issue resolution assuming that groups can identify their own interests. Accordingly, any explicit group demand will be regarded as a valid expression of that group's political interests in subsequent chapters.

Issues as a Source of Public Policy

We want to resolve social issues, but we also want the results to be "good public policy." These goals may often be incompatible; a policy that is good because it resolves a social issue may be bad when judged against other standards. Implicitly, at least, we ask whether a policy contributes to the achievement of common social purposes and whether it enhances widely held values in the society. For instance, a policy that increased racial inequality would be criticized regardless of any good points it might have. Unfortunately, the goals for policies are often themselves the basis for disagreement. How can we evaluate a policy that increases racial segregation while, let us say, furthering education and easing urban race confrontation? The single right answer necessary for policy judgment does not exist unless we impose a single arbitrary standard from among the many that may be put forward. The problem is not with the policy itself, but with the inconsistency among social goals.

Of course the American political process customarily "resolves" these irreconcilable judgments by compromise. In Charles E. Lindblom's well-known formulation, coordination occurs unconsciously through partisan mutual adjustment.[2] Policy changes proceed incrementally, and there may be great virtue in this when there is little chance of achieving an early, complete resolution of an issue. Failure to resolve an issue with each new increment does not invalidate existing policies bearing on the general problem. Indeed, it is the ability of all sides to take existing policy as given, and to proceed to bargain on that basis, that explains why the system may seem to work well and yet only rarely lay an issue completely to rest. In this regard, certain types of nonresolution may even lend legitimacy to existing policy, as when Supreme Court judges decline (but perhaps only temporarily!) to certify appeals from lower court rulings in a certain kind of case. The Supreme Court's refusal in 1977 to review the Gaylord case, in which Washington courts allowed the dismissal of a homosexual school teacher merely on the grounds of his affectional preference, cut short any hopes of expanding gay rights through judicial appeals.

Lindblom carries his analysis of partisan adjustment several steps further. The tentative and limited nature of the commitments made by all sides, he says, and the moderation imposed on all demands by the mutuality of the process contribute to greater agreement than could be achieved under a regime of central coordination. Value conflicts that would hobble a centralized, "rational" decision process cause no trouble in a system of partisan mutual adjustment because such a system does not assume the existence of a common interest or shared value.

It is incorrect, Lindblom argues, to praise democracy for its reliance on cooperative discussion, because such an approach often fails to produce agreement when participants cannot find a shared set of values against which they can measure proposed issue resolutions. Partisan discussion, in which the differing values of participants are revealed and consciously appealed to, is

---

[2] Charles E. Lindblom, *The Intelligence of Democracy,* New York, The Free Press, 1965.

to be preferred. In fact, the adjustment mechanisms offer a much better means of reaching a Pareto optimum (a position where no one can be benefited further without hurting someone else) by successive approximation than any centralized process could ever hope to.[3]

The implication of Lindblom's analysis is that issue resolution *does* produce good public policy, but only because issues are generally resolved in the United States through partisan mutual adjustment. The process itself should get the credit, and not the mere fact of issue resolution. By a series, typically, of partial resolutions it appears to draw off much of the energy that would have gone into complaints and attempts to undermine proposed solutions, and to turn that energy to constructive use in the search for more satisfactory policy.

Unfortunately, Lindblom's glowing appraisal of partisan mutual adjustment does not answer all the questions that might be raised. Adjustment occurs within the range of preferences held by the participants—any value not represented by them will not be served by any resolution they agree to. Mutual adjustment mechanisms may also deal harshly with interests caught in circumstances where their freedom to bargain is artificially constrained. For instance, draft reform can be debated in leisurely fashion in peacetime when the armed forces can be staffed by volunteers; when a national military mobilization is in progress, more urgency would be attached to prompt decision on a reformed draft system because every day multiplies the supposed injustice of the old system. Yet the draftees' bargaining power is not likely to be improved by an emergency mobilization.

Some issues may best be left alone, and here is a final situation in which issue resolution and good public policy may diverge. When government agencies are no better equipped to deal with a problem than private agencies, a bungled attempt at response can prematurely close an avenue of approach that might ultimately be the best response. No politician would want to advocate going further along a line already "proved" unworkable.

---

[3] Lindblom, *The Intelligence of Democracy*, Chapter 14.

The experience with the Head Start program supposedly showed that preschool enrichment for disadvantaged children does not help their school performance significantly. The Job Corps supposedly proved that intensive training and basic skills education for the hard core unemployed would not work well enough to be worth the expense. Yet these lessons were drawn in comparison with hypothetically superior programs that had not yet been developed, or with regard to more cost-effective uses for the same public funds in totally distinct policy areas. Neither the original program results nor the subsequent budgetary comparisons could possibly prove that Head Start was not the *most effective* educational program for disadvantaged kids, or that the Job Corps was not the *most effective* means of retrieving the hard core unemployed.

Neither program was very good in absolute terms, and it may have been valid to conclude in each instance that government agencies might just as well have stayed away from these problem areas, but this conclusion would not have solved either social problem. Is it appropriate to adopt a marginal program because it will show governmental commitment to resolving social issues? A poor policy may yet be the best means of resolving a social issue if it happens to be the best that can be done.

Politicians must decide whether the political gain implicit in government responsiveness is worth the cost of maintaining such a program. For Job Corps and Head Start they decided it wasn't, primarily because unrealistic expectations of dramatic success had been created before these programs went into effect. When the success did not materialize, the hoped-for political gains also soured. Even the good faith credits that politicians might have expected from a partial success were lost, and an "I told you so" reaction killed the programs.

Crisis, a subject to be explored in greater depth in Chapter 8, has some bearing on the acceptability of mediocre policies. In the 1930s, for instance, the WPA was defended as a concrete expression of governmental determination despite its mixed performance record. Perhaps if social intervention schemes of this magnitude are not oversold to begin with they will be more effective issue responses, even if no better as public policies. Perhaps also, careful experimentation with these strategies could have prevented a full-scale fiasco (see Chapter 3).

The Public Mood: Fat Years and Lean Years

The complexities of most social policy questions render any informed public judgment on government capacities almost impossible. Is the failure of a social strategy evidence of government incompetence? Why did the War on Poverty end with less than total victory? What lesson should be learned from the difficulties in government housing programs? Should we conclude from declining student test scores that governments are incapable of running an educational system? Is the inability of the federal government to maintain full employment and price stability simultaneously (or either one separately, for that matter) evidence that economic theories are unworkable as policy guides?

Every question in the last paragraph has been answered optimistically at times, and also pessimistically at times. The point is that governmental ability is subjectively dependent on public mood and experience, because public attitudes are often critical in mobilizing and directing national resources to the resolution of social issues. What we as a society decide we cannot do will not be done; what we decide we can do will have a much better chance of success.

In many ways, politics itself never changes. The same forces motivate or discourage individual politicians; the same calculus is used to prevent political wrong moves. Public attitudes are more variable, perhaps because they are formed more through rumor and hearsay than by direct experience of the political world. Over the years the public's fear of big government waxes and wanes relative to its apprehensions about big business and big labor. The fraction of the public having "a great deal of confidence" in the federal government, as measured by the Harris Poll, stood at 41% in 1966; by 1976 it had fallen to 11%, but by early 1977 (after the change of presidents) it had rebounded to 23%.[4] Similarly, government scores on keeping the peace and maintaining prosperity vary over time in ways that seem to reflect "public psychology" more than they do any observable changes in the real world.

Public confidence in government falls somewhere between David Easton's notions of "diffuse support" and "specific support" extended by the public to a political regime.[5] In this rather general form, Easton's important concepts are understandably hard to measure. Their importance has been confirmed, however, in one of the few areas where measurement can be made with some assurance, that of aggregate economic activity. George Katona's research into "psychological economics" shows that government performance in maintaining economic growth and price stability is reflected in high or low levels of consumer confidence.[6] In turn, consumer confidence influences consumer spending decisions, one of the major targets of government fiscal policy manipulations. Thus the public mood can have a strong effect on government success in specific policy areas.

The "extractive capability" of a government—the ease with which it can claim specific financial support from the public—shows a similar variability.[7] How much we can be taxed depends, within broad limits, on how much we are willing to forego, and for what purposes. The objective limits suggested by other mixed economies around the world are far higher than the 40% public sector currently found in the United States. Yet Swedish socialists lost their parliamentary majority in the 1976 elections over a plan to transfer ownership of major industries to groups of workers. In 1975, the British government was forced to back away from its 60% public sector level, despite resistance from the socialist wing of the majority Labour party, to avoid the inflationary and foreign consequences of heavy public spending. The British public probably cared little and understood less about the

---

[4] *Current Opinion,* **4,** V (1977), p. 37.

[5] David Easton, *A System Analysis of Political Life,* New York, John Wiley & Sons, 1965, pp. 268, 273–4.

[6] George Katona, *Psychological Economics,* New York, Elsevier, 1975.

[7] Gabriel A. Almond and G. Bingham Powell, Jr., *Comparative Politics: A Developmental Approach,* Boston, Little, Brown and Company, 1966, pp. 195–6.

size of the public sector, or even about British world prestige, than they did about inflation and their own tax burden. In the American context, high tax levels have been a popular political target for years, quite separate from the programs funded by those taxes. At the municipal level, especially, fiscal responsibility and a low tax ideology often dominate all other political issues. The rollback of California property taxes mandated by Proposition 13 passed in 1978 is another illustration of a "taxpayers' revolt" that went ahead with virtually no thought of its impact on public services.

Knowledge is the only essential for social issue resolution that cannot be replaced by public leadership, but even here some kind of response can occasionally proceed on the basis of ignorance, good intentions, and the blithe assumption that the job can be done one way or another. It sometimes seems that governments go through cycles of activism and quietism, or optimism and pessimism, correlated with the shifting state of expectations about government abilities. Public optimism supports governmental activism (although it may not be the prime cause of activism), while quietism is associated with (and may give rise to) pessimism about the ability to act effectively. A period of modest expectations naturally follows one of activism, for the results of activism are almost always less than completely satisfactory to everyone concerned. For their part, policy makers, whose political ambitions and enthusiasms may have played a substantial role in generating governmental overreaction (stretching knowledge and capacity beyond their limits) may overreact again and cut off marginal programs.

In short, the political acceptability of ambitious government efforts is a fragile commodity. Social and economic knowledge, tools, and financial support are necessary for governments to tackle certain kinds of social and economic problems, and without these resources politicians will be reluctant to admit the existence of difficult issues. Response to these issues may be encouraged by the availability of these resources, but temporary policy failures for whatever reason will again cast public doubt on government capacity.

The Public Mood: Appeals Against the Government

The federal government is already involved in most social issue areas even though direct governmental action may not logically be necessary for a resolution to occur. Thus the real policy choice is often that of more or less government involvement than at present, and the kind of involvement that will best serve social needs. In these circumstances there is always the danger that government action, intended as a positive step toward resolution of a social issue, may itself displace that issue. This is likely to happen if the governmental response becomes more controversial than the social problem to which it was addressed. The result is reemergence of the perennial government issue; the definition of the issue shifts from "what governmental response to this problem is most appropriate" to "how can we modify or eliminate this unwarranted government interference in social matters?"

School busing has something of this perverse character. Proponents of integrated schools initially responded with favor to school busing plans as a positive step to reduce the evils of segregated education, since it appeared impossible in the short run to change racially split housing patterns so that neighborhood schools would be inegrated "naturally." Difficulties in implementing busing plans, especially in northern urban areas, resulted in even greater controversy and more violent opposition to busing than had been directed toward segregated schools to begin with.

The perversity of this situation is twofold. First, the attempted resolution of a social issue has been pushed back one step because the controversy surrounding the governmental response itself must be resolved before the initial social problem can again be tackled. Second, opposition has solidified against a *governmental* solution, with the probable result that the legitimacy of governmental solutions to any problem has been undermined to some degree. By the nature of things, opposition cannot focus on "states of affairs" such as segregated schools, but only on actions or failures to act on the part of identifiable people, especially politicians. In taking on the school busing business and not succeeding quickly in implementing a solution, then, government leaders have turned an issue in which a minority (blacks) criticized a social situation and demanded corrective governmental action, into an issue in which a majority condemns and resists a specific governmental policy while offering no alternative way of resolving the underlying social issue.

Most social questions are not neutral with respect to the government issue. For any two competing issue positions, one will almost certainly call for more government involvement than the other, and the contrast will invoke the government issue to some degree. This fact is significant because many more people can be aroused by the government issue than by almost any other social concern. Further, an appeal against bloated government is often a conscious political strategy; it is an effort to bring into the conflict those groups whose opposition to governmental expansion is only latent, and who could not be mobilized to take part in a similar controversy based only on a substantive policy issue.

The government issue is inherently biased; when circumstances are favorable for raising it, it can be a potent source of opposition to particular proposals irrespective of their substantive merits. In circumstances favorable to government expansion—wartime, the New Deal period in the 1930s, the New Frontier and the Great Society of the 1960s—appeals against the government are ineffective because broad public majorities place an almost blind trust in their political leaders. Barry Goldwater, the Republican presidential candidate in 1964, encountered something of this reaction with his proposals to dismantle the Tennessee Valley Authority, cut back on Social Security payments programs, and in other ways return power to state and local governments. These appeals were nonissues, or perhaps it might be said that they called up the losing side of previously resolved versions of the government issue. Goldwater's strategy was predicted on a silent majority that opposed big government, but to many groups across the country it must have appeared that his approach would halt progressive legislative responses to a number of problems just as they were getting started.

In periods of entrenchment—the immediate post World War II years, the early 1970s—disillusioned majorities actually do distrust politics, fear the expansion of already big government, and resist any proposal likely to invade their privacy or abridge their freedoms any further. The anti-Washington sentiment that came to the surface in the 1976 elections, nourished by the Vietnam war, social policy failures of the 1960s, Watergate, sex scandals in government, high taxes, inflation, unemployment, presidential rhetoric and the energy crisis, illustrates the sweeping uncritical hostility to government that can sometimes be tapped by properly phrased appeals.

Thus the government issue is not a phony issue, for all that its most prominent propagandists may often be self-serving when they invoke it. It is valid as a procedural matter, quite apart from the substantive circumstances in which it arises, because large numbers of citizens evaluate proposals on these grounds, and they have a stake in the extension of government power whether any proposed extension will affect them directly or not. The inability of any democratic regime to prevent public debate on policy controversies, even if it tried, creates a presumption for accepting the government issue at face value. More positively, the possible precedent-setting effects of extensions of government power give all citizens a strong and unquestioned interest in the scope of government, even though widespread exercise of this prerogative may hamstring the issue translation process.

Politicians and Conflict

It would be misleading, in a book on social issues, to regard all of politics as inherently conflictual. There is no question that much political action takes place in response to one-sided demands made on policymakers, with no effective counterdemand present. At the same time, lack of opposition does not guarantee success. It is useful to look briefly at the kinds of questions handled without overt conflict, and also to see how politicians react to the "joining" of an issue. The situation is more complex than it might seem at first: some nonconflictual demands are not met, but politicians may sometimes have reason to go in search of new issues while they are still only latent. The significance of these political predispositions will be amplified later in the examination of specific issues.

In the first place, politicians may prefer to turn down some requests, whether conflictual or not, to increase the value of those requests they do agree to. Further, politicians may turn down some requests for which they have every reason to expect gratitude if they did grant the request. The asked-for response may be costly, for instance. It may disrupt budgetary calculations, or it may put a strain on the politician's political position even if it does not excite overt controversy.

Politicians often find themselves in a dilemma. They do not want to get a reputation as a soft touch, for this may damage their credibility with the general public—the voters—hence they resist giving in easily. At the same time, they often prefer to resolve potential conflicts by denying the existence of irreconcilable differences and responding separately to each request as it is received. This strategy, when it is successful, compartmentalizes and privatizes political response, but also limits its scope as well. It privatizes response by treating interest group demands essentially as matter for resolution by private contract between politicians and group leaders. The distinction between this and true private contractual arrangements—that here the government official's promises are made good with public rather than personal funds—seems to go unnoticed by parties to the agreement.

The politician's instinct to "treat" separately with each claimant limits the scope of response by concentrating efforts on those policies susceptible to ready division among a number of claimants. Thus pork barrel spending, contracts, and tax loopholes are favored kinds of responses when they are even halfway appropriate to the demand. A response to claimants solely according to their status (see Chapter 8) is a similar approach. As the work of Theodore Lowi and others shows,[8] the aggregate size of

[8] Theodore J. Lowi, *The End of Liberalism*, New York, W.W. Norton, 1969.

such responses tends to increase without obvious limit, but politicians are usually shielded from political harm because the aggregate is hidden, its growth is incremental, and no single addition is greatly controversial in itself.

So the circumstances in which a single demand or pressure can be exerted successfully and without opposition are not unimportant by any means. Many such demands are agreed to, many more are compromised with available financial resources or political capital, and some few are rejected outright (in favor of doing nothing rather than doing something else specific) every year, all without becoming embroiled in political issue controversies. Political institutions are designed in part to suppress issues by avoiding the seemingly obvious facts that policies depend for their success on the exercise of governmental power, that they cost money or other scarce resources, and that they tend to be zero sum—for each winner there is almost always a loser. When these facts are recognized, especially by the potential losers, the conditions for a social issue are present.

Politicians as Heroes?

So far we have touched only the constraints on government activity imposed by vague public feelings of optimism or pessimism about the capacity of government to respond to social issues. There is no reason to believe that all politicians are always constrained by public timidity. Surely there is some scope for political leadership, but how much?

Politicians are unquestionably hampered by having a personal stake in doing the right thing politically. We as citizens try to place our elected leaders in this position, and we are often urged to make their lives even more difficult by insisting that they take stands and offer real choices on the issues. We create for them the strong likelihood of a conflict between doing what they feel is for the public good and doing what they feel is in their own interest as career politicians. When conflict does occur—when elected representatives believe their constituents are wrong in their opinions or have taken too narrow a view of the issues (although the constituents may perceive their own interests correctly)—politicians must choose to support their constituents, turn against them and then hope they forget, try to persuade them they were wrong, or decide to take their lumps at the next election.

This conflict is built into the system, and is to some degree desirable and necessary. If politicians never paid any attention to the possibility of losing votes by their actions, they would not be under even the slight measure of electoral control that now prevails. But if politicians always followed their constituencies and never responded to their own sense of what is right and wrong, they would be superfluous and held in low esteem by the citizenry. To show themselves reasonably balanced and worthy of having their decisions ratified, they must sometimes go along with their constituents and sometimes go out on a limb instead.

The constituency constraint is obvious in principle but not so in practice. To begin with, most elected politicians believe that they are faithful representatives of their constituencies. Unfortunately, they represent only their own perception of constituency opinion, and this perception is often incorrect, especially for issues of low salience to the constituency. John W. Kingdon's research provides the best picture of the behavior of politicians under political constraint.[9] Among members of Congress, Kingdon finds individual attitudes parallel those of the constituency about 75% of the time. Further, the constituency is a gatekeeper for a variety of other interests. Politicians are concerned not so much about each individual vote as they are about having a ready explanation—"excuse" might be a better word— for every major vote on which they expect constituency opposition. At all costs they seek to avoid a "string of votes" against their constituents, a goal that should not be too difficult to achieve because conflict between their vote intention and constituency opinion occurs less than 20% of the time according to Kingdon. In general, then, American elected politicians appear to conform to constituency expectations without feeling compel-

[9] John W. Kingdon, *Congressmen's Voting Decisions,* New York, Harper and Row, 1973. See also John W. Kingdon, *Candidates for Office: Beliefs and Strategies,* New York, Random House, 1966.

led by them. There is ample room for independent behavior of several kinds.

First, representatives may decide to throw their own weight on the scales because a position taken by an issue public coincides with their own personal goals or preferences. There are political dangers here, but probably less severe ones than those incurred by taking a stand that is known to be disapproved by a popular majority. The real problem in either case is the strong possibility of antagonizing one's fellow politicians. Genuine personal belief and commitment is usually respected among politicians, but the respect granted to it diminishes with the possibility that such commitment may influence the outcome of a social issue.

Being a maverick is tolerated best, whether in legislative setting or in administrative circles, when it is seen as harmless (and ineffectual) eccentricity. Exercise of political will is a completely safe enterprise only for those politicians who are in a powerful enough position to exercise their will without fear of reprisal, or for those politicians who are not concerned greatly about their political future. At best, political willfulness in this context is likely to be viewed as arrogance by fellow politicians, at worst it may be regarded as a devious trick to undermine the legitimate expression of the other side of the question. Fanatics on issues such as abortion or gun control, for example, often present their own views, and sometimes discuss the issue in such absolute terms that compromise positions can scarcely be presented.

Far-sighted politicians may anticipate the direction an issue will take and act in advance of public sentiment. But the course of an issue may be anticipated incorrectly, and the far-sighted politician may take a position that later turns out to be unpopular. Another possibility is that the issue may disappear spontaneously. The politician will then be left with an unnecessary position or project in hand and a debt resulting from the expenditure of political capital for an unneeded end. Finally, the response to the anticipated issue may not work correctly, again leaving the politician holding the bag, and what is worse, credited with an unnecessary failure.

Despite the dangers, the rewards for anticipating issues are

compelling enough that a substantial number of elected politicians seek out issues to display their ability to deal with them. To
anticipate a problem successfully contributes to a statesmanlike
image, to a reputation for success, to widespread publicity and
recognition. Louis W. Koenig (among other scholars) suggests
that political career ambitions are a powerful incentive for politicians to play the role of issue entrepreneur.[10] Carried to its
extreme, this goes far beyond simple passive receptivity to new
ideas. The approach is popular in Congress, especially in the
Senate, where a number of ambitious presidential hopefuls regularly do battle with each other. Senatorial staff are often assigned to specific topic areas and given the task of directing a
Senator's career through a constructive choice of committee assignments and issue concerns.

Committee assignments are especially useful as springboards
because they do deal only with restricted subject areas (on which
a Senator can more easily be made to look sagacious) and they
allow a Senator to orient public statements toward a hand-picked
national constituency—a latent issue public, perhaps, waiting to
be mobilized by the appearance of favorable government response. Committee assignments, especially subcommittee and
committee chairmanships, bring with them control over committee staff and the further opportunity to arrange hearings and
hold press conferences designed to show concern for particular
social issues.

Both houses of Congress are limited by statute in the number
of committees they may create, but not in the number of possible
subcommittees. The obvious result, coincident with the desires
of members of both houses to multiply the number of positions
of leverage on public opinion, has been a dramatic increase in
the number of subcommittees and special and select committees
in both houses. Prior to the 1977 Senate committee reforms, the
tally stood at 139 subcommittees for the Senate's 24 committees
and 146 subcommittees for 28 committees in the House. The
rate of growth of subcommittees has averaged two per house per

---

[10] Louis W. Koenig, *Congress and the President,* Glenview, Ill., Scott, Foresman and
Co., 1965, p. 16.

year since the 1946 Legislative Reorganization Act took effect. A glance at the titles of past Senate select committees will suggest their nature: Select Government Intelligence Gathering Activities, Select Nutrition and Human Needs, Select Small Business, Special Committee on Aging, Special Committee on National Emergencies and Delegated Emergency Powers.

When will politicians avoid conflict, and when will they seek it out? Surprisingly little is known about individual political motivations. Richard Fenno's extensive study of congressmen in committees[11] shows that some value "good public policy" and gravitate toward committees where they can debate social issues and take strong stands. Those legislators seeking reelection above all else look for a committee with an easily pleased constituency organization. But we cannot tell in advance what will motivate any particular individual, and we can't even say whether the policy process needs more of one kind of politician or another. The work of James David Barber[12] has considerably advanced our knowledge of the psychological quirks and predispositions of presidents, and how these are reflected in presidential operating style and response to political crisis, but it must also be said that presidents are often unusual people. How far Barber's approach, developed in a study of presidents, could apply to politicians in less exalted positions, remains to be tested.

This brief treatment of the impact of individual politicians on the issue translation process concludes by pointing to some possible pitfalls. For example, overeager politicians may do the political process a disservice if they respond to an issue prematurely and without knowing whether the problem can be handled successfully or not. Committee hearings can be dead ends, never resulting in a committee report or specific legislative proposal, but at the same time harrassing executive agencies and galvanizing interest groups into actions that may prove fruitless. A politician's personal failure to carry through a line of inquiry

[11] Richard F. Fenno, Jr., *Congressmen in Committees,* Boston, Little, Brown and Company, 1973.
[12] James David Barber, *The Presidential Character: Predicting Performance in the White House,* Second Edition, Englewood Cliffs, N.J., Prentice-Hall, 1977.

may cast doubt on the credibility of the entire governmental apparatus if it raises false hopes. Inexperienced lobby groups may be disillusioned when the mere holding of hearings on a particular social issue fails to put the issue high on the governmental agenda. "Don't deal with a problem until it forces itself upon you" might be a good motto for the cautious politician, but cautious politicians don't (usually) get to be president.

Presidents feel similar political limitations. As a representative, the president supposedly reflects a broad national constituency. In practice, this often means that the president represents a series of smaller social groups with their own disparate concerns, because the most concerned sector of the public shifts from issue to issue. The blue ribbon commission and other techniques in the standard repertoire of presidential information gathering devices are all susceptible to the danger of raising false hopes among potential issue publics. A commission on income maintenance alternatives, for instance, will attract the attention of welfare rights groups and put pressure on the president to recommend some plan similar to that chosen by the commission. If no plan is forthcoming, the issue public will feel betrayed, commission members will be disgruntled that their careful work was disregarded, and the president will get a black eye for "playing politics" with the welfare issue.

In recent years it has proved so difficult for presidents to get outside information without feeling pressured to act on it immediately, that they have often gone underground, asking for recommendations from outside advisory committees and brain trusts, but imposing strict secrecy on the nature of the recommendations. Many are still set aside for reasons known only to the president, but there is no artificially generated political pressure to respond constructively to every issue area being investigated, members of the advisory committees are not slighted publicly, and the president can fix the nature and timing of recommended governmental response, and even attempt to redefine the issue, according to his own political calculations. In reality, however, when Presidents Kennedy and Johnson used this technique they found that other policy commitments like the Berlin crisis, the Vietnam war, tax cuts and surcharges, and splits within the Democratic party thoroughly scrambled any strategic planning they might have done.[13]

This last example should remind us again of the severe political constraints often imposed by the coincident occurrence of a large number of social issues. The balky nature of our political institutions, especially the pervasiveness of public sentiments, shows most clearly when a number of social issues come in conflict with one another. The next chapter considers the impact of more specific governmental institutions and procedures—do they aid the resolution of social issues, or do they themselves contribute to the problem?

---

[13] E. Ray Canterbery, *Economics on a New Frontier,* Belmont, Calif., Wadsworth Publishing Company, 1968; Robert Warren Stevens, *Vain Hopes, Grim Realities: The Economic Consequences of the Vietnam War,* New York, Franklin Watts, 1976.

3

Problems and Solutions: In Search of Good Policy

What Is the Problem?

Beyond political will, the first requirement for effective governmental response is governmental intelligence. If response to an issue is to be grounded in reality, policy makers must know what the basic social or economic problem is and what its possible solutions might be. As Charles E. Lindblom observes, problems are not "given."[1] Someone must define even those problems that seem familiar to everyone. Issue publics cannot be assumed to know exactly what is wrong, nor can they be expected to provide useful, unbiased analyses of existing policies or policy options. Even the most highly organized groups usually react just to the immediate symptoms of social problems, whose causes are unknown. They express concern about a problem without pretending to diagnose it or prescribe remedies based on extensive research. Where interest groups do maintain their own research arm, its purpose is to marshall evidence for the group's traditional points of view, and to provide ammunition for the group's political allies.

Whatever form it takes, some means of governmental issue analysis is essential. Nearly every social problem these days is

[1] Charles E. Lindblom, *The Policy-Making Process,* Englewood Cliffs, N.J., Prentice-Hall, Inc., 1965, p. 13.

sufficiently complex and its causes so well concealed that the solution, or indeed the problem itself, are not self-evident. As issues are joined, competing definitions of the problem are added, each definition being advanced by a different group and each definition implying a somewhat different solution. The entire process is thoroughly politicized, in other words, and government policy makers will hope in vain for the "correct" definition of the problem and its solution to rise to the top automatically. The definition advanced with the most persuasive force, or the most plausible solution, certainly cannot be assumed to be the most nearly correct.

More important, no single approach may be more nearly correct than the others, either objectively or because it is more likely to resolve the overall issue. The results of decades of social science research show that the complexity of social issues is usually real, and not just political. Some combination of the various issue positions may be needed, both objectively and politically, but there may be so much uncertainty that no approach can be deemed superior with any degree of confidence. Yet despite objective uncertainty, political pressures often may dictate that some definition of the issue be adopted so that government agencies may proceed to implement a solution.

Debates over welfare reform illustrate uncertainty in a typically complex social issue area. In the 1960s, the immediate problem arose in a bureaucratic context. City and state welfare agencies were dismayed at the rising case loads and growing welfare fraud in programs such as Aid to Families with Dependent Children. Taxpayers were angered by the rapidly rising cost of welfare. Reformers were unhappy about low benefit levels, red tape, invasion of privacy, the breakdown of welfare families, and the unavailability of aid to the working poor.[2] A variety of reform proposals directed themselves to one problem or another: flat income guarantees, various kinds of negative income tax, streamlining of welfare administration, job training, work tests, children's allowances, modifications to the food

---

[2] Committee for Economic Development, *Improving the Public Welfare System*, New York, Committee for Economic Development, 1970.

stamps program, more public housing, better inner city education. To adopt just one of these proposals would be to deny the complexity of the problem, but to attempt to fit new programs to new sets of beneficiaries would perpetuate the discredited categoric aid approach and bloat the welfare bureaucracy even further.[3]

Uncertainty and disagreement of this magnitude will slow political processes, but there are at least two general methods for choosing a working definition of a social issue like welfare reform ("how can the effectiveness of welfare aid programs be improved?"). One method is governmental preemption of the issue. The appropriate government agency may simply declare that it has identified the major problem for current attention, and that it is proceeding with further steps to implement this viewpoint. When successful, this approach short circuits the elaborate issue definition process outlined in Chapter 4. The other major approach is similar—it involves a strong, albeit indirect, measure of governmental influence in the issue definition process (for an example, see the discussion of teenage unemployment in Chapter 1).

In both these instances, government intelligence "clout" may be more critical than government intelligence per se. The ability to produce a credible, authoritative definition of the issue and impose it on the confusion produced by competing issue publics may be more fruitful than trying to find the one right definition. From the government's viewpoint, there is an additional reason to be involved even if it is not possible to preempt the issue. Recall that the initial premise of this discussion was that there is little meaning to the "correct" definition of an issue. When this is true, it is rational for government officials to influence the redefinition of the issue in directions they are best prepared to deal with. Lacking such influence, policy makers may be faced with an issue to which they cannot easily respond with success.

Attempted government preemption usually gives one kind of policy solution an inside track over the remaining hurdles in the

---

[3] These problems are reviewed in Peter Marris and Martin Rein, *Dilemmas of Social Reform,* New York, Atherton Press, 1967.

policy process, and issue publics should be quick to respond to these cues. Proposal of a Family Assistance Plan by the Nixon administration in 1969 indicated the administration's willingness to consider those aspects of the welfare problem associated with the working poor. Reform proponents could then redirect their attention to this view of the issue. Unfortunately, opponents found the subsidiary issue of work incentives boldly highlighted by the administration's plan, and they redirected their attack to this vulnerable spot. Issue redefinition mobilizes opponents as well as supporters.

FAP was not a success story, but it illustrates another significant feature of governmental preemption of issue definitions. In proposing FAP, the Nixon administration indicated that it was willing to be held accountable for the results of implementing the program. Where issue demands are not clear, or even logical, political accountability must allow for an adequate measure of political leadership as well. There is little sense in holding policy makers accountable to public confusion, as would be the case if they merely cobbled together a solution from the conflicting public viewpoints on welfare or any other complex social issue.

Government Intelligence: Counting Noses

The development of social monitoring abilities is important to issue definition because it offers a means for policy makers to anticipate issues and, where objective facts are relevant to the identification of issues, it is an asset in asserting a single authoritative statement of the problem at hand. But Americans have become increasingly suspicious of government information-gathering schemes, regarding them as a kind of Big Brother invasion of privacy. It is for this reason, perhaps, that most governmental policy making relies on nongovernmental information sources or on ad hoc information gathering by means such as Congressional committee hearings. Legislative committees do not generate their own information. When they sponsor hearings, external interest groups and executive agencies present evidence from their own sources. Often the hearings have been arranged to publicize and lend support to a prior conclusion reached within the committee, suggesting that external information comes too late to change committee decisions. The same can be said of legislative staff research and investigatory hearings. Tentative decisions have often been made before the research is set in motion.

The most detailed information on public programs comes from the executive agencies already operating in the area. This information is incomplete, however, because it usually treats just the results of current programs. True, the evidence comes from some form of monitoring, but it is program monitoring rather than social monitoring. Normal social changes and the effects of the program confound each other and make separation of the program's independent effects impossible. Program monitoring can answer many questions about the program itself, but not about the need for related or substitute programs.[4]

What is the federal government's present capacity for societal monitoring? Several monitoring devices are important today, and a variety of recent proposals have suggested substantial refinements of this capability, but it is still generally true that little societal monitoring occurs for its own sake. Specific purposes lie behind most monitoring efforts, and the statistics produced by these projects must be examined carefully for potential limitations in their applicability to other problems and policies.

The decennial census of the United States, first conducted in 1790, was begun for the limited purpose of apportioning seats in the House of Representatives. Over the years, however, it has acquired a number of significant (although secondary) purposes which have been, in some instances, at odds with the legislative apportionment task. The census of population has included variables such as age, family status, race and national origin, occupation and income, work experience, physical mobility, and at one time even religion. Thus it has chronicled the influx of immigrants, settlement of the West, patterns of segregation and

---

[4] See generally Carol H. Weiss, *Evaluation Research,* Englewood Cliffs, N.J., Prentice-Hall, Inc., 1972.

racial and ethnic prejudice, urbanization and suburbanization, poverty, and the rise and decline of the farmer and the indust- rial era in the United States. For interpreters of the grand sweep of history, the decennial census has been a splendid instrument, but serious questions may be raised about its usefulness in the year-by-year choice and assessment of public policies. At most, it may serve to provide benchmarks for the measurement of long- term trends in society. It is too crude to serve as a source of information about short-term trends in social problems, and to- tally unable to help in the task of measuring policy impacts.

Special quinquennial censuses have grown up alongside the census of population to address special questions—a census of manufactures, a census of business, a census of housing, a census of state and local governments. These have filled some gaps, but they are still severely limited by their adherence to the enumera- tion principle, an approach which can answer only questions of the type "how many of x are there in the country?" One fruitful alternative to the enumeration approach (required for legislative apportionment) is the sample survey. With the development of reliable national sampling methods following World War II, sig- nificant census-type questions could be asked much more often—yearly, for instance—and at substantially lower cost. The yearly series of Current Population Reports on the poverty population, begun in 1959, is an excellent example of this ap- proach. This series uses sampling techniques to uncover sig- nificant trends in the age, race and sex composition of the poor within the time period normally elapsing between one census and the next. It has also collected valuable data on work experi- ence, size of income deficit by family, and sources of poor family income on a yearly basis. These data have been critical in shap- ing informed opinion on welfare reform and income mainte- nance proposals.[5]

It has been symptomatic of the pluralism of American gov- ernment that official sources of social statistics have multiplied, and that a new agency or new policy problem often calls forth a new statistical series. The most famous example of this

---

[5] The report cited in footnote 2 made prominent use of these statistics.

phenomenon is the national unemployment rate, which was created in the 1930s as a means of measuring the severity of the depression. The other well-known product of the Bureau of Labor Statistics, the consumer price index, has a similar rationale. It is used extensively in labor-management negotiations as a measure of increases in the cost of living, and, together with BLS surveys of wage rates and working conditions, it helps to establish the prevailing wage rates that federal contracts are legally obligated to match.

Social Indicators

The inadequacy of existing social statistics, and their spotty character, nourished a "social indicator" or "social accounting" movement in the late 1960s and early 1970s.[6] In many respects the idea was an appealing one, but reactions to it revealed some of the political undercurrents in questions of government intelligence. The volume "Toward a Social Report" published in January 1969 by the Secretary of Health, Education and Welfare of the outgoing Johnson Administration, suggested the regular collection of a variety of statistics on the nation's social well-being, measuring such things as life expectancy, family stability, rates of political participation, poverty and income inequality, artistic activity, racial differentials in educational attainment, and crime. Bills introduced in the Senate by Walter Mondale (D–Minn.), which were the subject of hearings in 1970, proposed the creation of a Council of Social Advisers (paralleling the existing Council of Economic Advisers) charged with preparing such a social report each year and recommending to the President courses of action to remedy any weak spots shown by the reports.

There never was much public or governmental support for the Social Report idea, and it encountered significant opposition from politicians who thought its implications not to their liking. The implicit assumption of the Social Report is that social problems exist, cannot be solved without government intervention,

---

[6] Raymond A. Bauer, ed., *Social Indicators,* Cambridge, MIT Press, 1966.

and should be met by appropriate government actions. Conservative politicians tended to regard this as some kind of Democratic or liberal trick, especially since a Democratic incumbent had just been forced to give up his reelection plans and his would-be Democratic successor (Hubert Humphrey) had lost the election. The existence of such a report in a Republican administration would have been a continuing embarrassment because it could be interpreted as a call for policies that Republicans had no intention of passing. Actually, a social report would probably have been an embarrassment to either party because it would have implied governmental willingness to respond far beyond the actual capacity of any government.

A final problem with social indicators would have surfaced after the system had been in operation for some while. Such indicators are usually broad enough to obscure the effects of any one policy, and so they cannot be used to assess individual policy impact. In truth, they are not very useful in assigning causal connections of any sort. At best, they can focus attention on a social problem, but by themselves they cannot show whether existing policies aid or exacerbate a problem perceived by the public, nor can they show whether a new policy would be better than the current one.

Some of these problems can be illustrated by another well-known national statistic, the series of Uniform Crime Reports compiled by the FBI from data submitted by local law enforcement agencies. This series regularly produces scary statistics of rampant crime, which are then cited as authoritative evidence by advocates of stronger crime control measures and bigger law enforcement budgets. There is no question that the Uniform Crime Reports are authoritative; there is considerable question what they mean and how, if at all, valid inferences can be drawn from them. A closer look at this one indicator may serve to illuminate some general difficulties with social indicators and some serious limitations on their usefulness in the resolution of public issues.[7]

To begin with, the FBI reports include only those crimes

---

[7] This discussion draws upon Albert D. Biderman, "Social Indicators and Goals," in Bauer, ed., *Social Indicators,* pp. 111–29.

known to the police, because the police provide the figures. Sample surveys of crime victimization quite regularly turn up claimed levels of criminal activity several times higher than that reported to law enforcement agencies. Is there a bias to non-reporting? Of course there is. Crimes against the person, with the exception of rape, are much more likely to be reported than crimes against property. Less than one case of fraud out of four becomes a criminal statistic, while more than half of all robberies are known by police.[8]

The reported crime rate in some cities is surprisingly low. The reason for the low rates may lie in selective reporting by the police, and it may also lie in selective complaining by victims. If they expect no police response, they are unlikely to take the time to report crimes against themselves. Crimes by blacks against blacks are notoriously underreported.

Second, the Uniform Crime Reports invite lumping together of all types of crime (not numbers of criminals) in order to produce a single "crime rate," whose fluctuations from year to year make neat concise headlines (generally justifying increased law enforcement expenditures). The public does not feel equally alarmed or equally threatened by all forms of crime, yet the reports it is asked to interpret make distinctions difficult.

Third, and perhaps most serious for possible policy making uses, there is an inherent ambiguity in the interpretation of trends in the crime statistics. Improved police practices almost always produce higher reported crime rates, because crimes are more often reported to the police, and more often reported by the police when they are known. Yet it seems perverse to argue, on the basis of this evidence, that a higher reported crime rate is a good thing, for a higher reported rate might also have resulted from higher actual incidence of criminal activity. Similarly, by itself a small drop in the crime rate may say nothing about the effectiveness of newly adopted police techniques, and studies where changes in crime rate *can* be linked to changes in police practice almost never show dramatic crime rate drops.

[8] The first national victimization survey was sponsored by the President's Commission on Law Enforcement and Administration of Justice. See the Commission's report, *The Challenge of Crime in a Free Society,* New York, Avon Books, 1968, p. 96ff.

The Search for Techniques

The issue translation process rarely proceeds step by step from issue definition to the choice of a public policy solution, even though it is convenient to analyze the process in these discrete segments. More commonly, the definition of an issue is influenced strongly by the available means of response; that is, basically, by habitual ways of thinking. This section looks at governmental techniques and at recent efforts to expand the list of available policy responses.

The number of distinct kinds of government activity is not large, although the variety of bureaucratic changes that can be rung on these few types is truly amazing. Figure 1 shows two lists of governmental inputs and outputs, indicating the range of governmental activity. The effectiveness of any of these techniques is situational—it *may* work if it is applied to the right problem at the right time and in the right manner. A great many government projects, past and present, demonstrate that success is highly conditional indeed and depends on knowing what to do and on actually doing it right. The lists in Figure 1 suggest both kinds of problem.

"Knowing what to do" will, in some instances, require the assumption that the appropriate targets for regulation or for aid can be identified. But those legally entitled to aid do not always come forward. Welfare programs have often demonstrated this problem, and welfare rights organizations have been able to put great strain on traditional categoric aid programs like AFDC simply by informing eligible women of their rights and helping them claim the benefits to which they are legally entitled. At the other end of the income scale, many tax lawyers make good money for themselves and their clients by seeking out all the loopholes to which their clients might legally stake a claim. In neither example can it be said with certainty what percentage of the eligible category has taken advantage of its rights.

Proliferation of reporting paperwork causes problems in both benefit and regulatory policies. Regulatees often manage to avoid regulators by failing to file forms, or by failing to comply with the substance of regulation, which will also not be known until duly recorded by an inspector checking up on compliance.

Figure 1:   What can governments do?

On the input side: Investigate
                     Register
                     Require reporting
                     Jail
                     Borrow money
                     Impose taxes
                     Contract for
                     Hire and pay

On the output side: Exhort, directly or in the name of the public
                     Prohibit, including criminalize
                     Establish minimum standards (quality, quantity)
                     License and certify
                     Issue cease and desist orders
                     Mediate, conciliate, arbitrate, adjudicate, coordinate
                     Discourage by taxation
                     Reduce or underwrite risks
                     Guarantee profits
                     Lend money
                     Give grants
                     Make transfer payments
                     Provide in-kind benefits
                     Inform, study, and publicize
                     Extend legal protection
                     Manage services

Benefit-seekers are deterred or delayed by having to fill out forms, and a decision on their request must then wait for processing of their application.

Knowing what to do in regulatory policy often means knowing the right regulatory target. But controlling one supposed critical part of a larger social or economic process sometimes simply reveals another level that must also be regulated. In its efforts to control price increases in food, especially meat, the Nixon administration imposed price controls on retail sales in

1971. A somewhat shadowy group of "middlemen," assumed to be making large profits, was blamed for price rises. When price controls produced shortages in the supermarket, however, food prices were decontrolled at the same time that the strict Phase III-B freeze was reimposed on all other sectors of the economy. The "middlemen" were real enough, but the markup imposed by each fell short of the windfall profits that would have allowed—and justified—effective regulation.

Grants, loans, and transfer payments assume that a shortage of money in the hands of local governments, farmers, the unemployed and disabled is the root cause of their problems, and that more demand will stimulate the supply of goods and services needed by these beneficiary groups. But demand may not immediately or automatically bring forth supply. Money in the hands of home buyers will stimulate housing construction only if builders and construction unions are inclined to cooperate; school districts can use their aid funds effectively only if the appropriate qualified staff can be found, preferably unemployed, unattached, and willing to move to their new job site at once.

Knowing how to stimulate economic growth often involves assuming the existence of financial entrepreneurs and industrial risk-takers. But it may be impossible to lure them away from lucrative investment opportunities to take advantage of government investment credits and loan guarantees; or there may simply not be enough of them to matter.

Building Bureaucracies

The biggest trick of the government trade is program administration. Whether the program's agents are private actors coopted for the purpose, as with doctors and Medicare, or government employees, as in the Food and Drug Administration, they are enmeshed in a complex bureaucratic net handling a large number of individual cases every year. Every one of the activities listed in Figure 1 depends on a large bureaucracy—to process tax returns, issue Social Security checks, respond to requests for information, apprehend and try criminal suspects, feed the Pentagon's computers, inspect air pollution controls, license power plants, supply defense bases, shred obsolete records, and for all the other activities of government agencies for which human beings have so far proved indispensable.

The costs of regulatory protection are substantial even when government agencies are not involved in grant programs. The Food and Drug Administration costs more than $200 million a year to run, for example, air pollution control and occupational safety and health programs both cost more than $100 million a year, and even the lowly Interstate Commerce Commission spends more than $50 million a year. Coordination costs money too. The Executive Office of the President employs about 5000 people, and Congress employs 25,000. Congress is a $1 billion business although it spends virtually nothing actually adminstering policy.

The need for bureaucratic organization, and the problems associated with it, will be found in any large organization. The principles of division of labor, allocation of functions and responsibilities, and hierarchical supervision have been known and applied intuitively for a long time—at least as long as the United States has been in existence. Judged by the standards of its time, the United States federal government has always been a large organization, hence it has always needed a substantial bureaucracy. This apparatus has grown in response to growing case loads in each department and in consequence of a marked expansion of functions over the years. From this perspective, the expansion of bureaucracy has proceeded at an increasing rate, although not greatly out of line with population growth or increases in national economic output. Americans are decidedly suspicious of bureaucracy, however. Population growth and level of Gross National Product are not the accepted standards for measuring the size of bureaucratic enterprise. Every additional government employee means a new "all-time high" and every additional dollar for staff puts the bureaucracy at a "record spending" level, regardless of the size of case load or the expansion of functions offered.

There is no trick to expanding a government bureaucracy, if Congress can be persuaded to appropriate the funds. There will always be applicants, and hiring then even helps reduce unemployment! The government does not make a profit, so it cannot have a loss either, no matter how much deadwood it takes on (and the civil service merit system established by the Pendleton Act in 1883 does not insist that those hired be fully qualified, only that they be the best among the applicants). Only if agency personnel directors care about the effectiveness of their agency can we expect that an effort will be made to get and keep the best personnel.

The question of size itself is not the important one, however, because the expansion of functions and the increase in case loads render any judgment of the proper size of the bureaucracy fruitless. Critics of bureaucracy per se, even those sympathetic to the regulatory and welfare programs that have been responsible for its recent expansion, fear that its growth is the occasion for inefficiency and that growth feeds on itself. A large part of this question is the matter of economies and diseconomies of scale. So-called learning curves for bureaucratic organizations show that each additional case added to the case load is handled more cheaply than the average cost of the current case load.[9] Organizations too small to take advantage of computer technology will usually be more costly than large ones that are computerized. And so on. But beyond some point there may be diseconomies of scale that begin to outweigh the advantages of size. For instance, central purchasing may result in lower average purchase prices, but eventually the increased cost of distribution from a central storehouse may eat up the benefits of volume purchasing. Centralized personnel services will probably be cheaper than decentralized, but beyond some point the centralized apparatus may lose touch with the peculiar needs of each unit for which it hires, resulting in less effective hiring decisions.

Where diseconomies of scale start is not clearly known, but an enterprise with 2,982,000 civilian employees, as the federal government had in 1970, must experience some increasing costs.

---

[9] Empirical studies are surveyed in Leonard Merewitz and Stephen H. Sosnick, *The Budget's New Clothes,* Chicago, Markham Publishing Company, 1971, pp. 231–5.

How can these inefficiencies be prevented, while still preserving the essential benefits of the bureaucratic form—impartiality and strict adherence to rules? Of course it is misleading to think of the entire three million falling under a single hierarchical chain of command. Many work for the independent regulatory commissions and are therefore removed from presidential control, others work for the legislative and judicial branches, still others are political appointees hired outside the civil service rules, and a very large group is the army of clerks and typists whose skills are largely interchangeable across a great many agencies.

Nevertheless the federal bureaucracy has reached the point, even with the differentiation just mentioned, where decision making is overly cumbersome. A symptom of this is the efforts of the Nixon administration to decentralize policy making in the major departments on a geographic basis, eliminating much of the former necessity for each department to clear its actions with Washington before applying them within a geographic region of the country. This approach certainly helps, but it can probably succeed only in bringing the effectiveness of the bureaucracy back to the level it displayed when it was smaller and more compact. There are definite—if unknown—limits to the size of an efficient bureaucracy, and the federal government is pushing those limits now.

Keeping Them Under Control

To be fair to the critics of governmental growth, they are worried about something more important than a little inefficiency. Their concern with a bloated bureaucracy is that it will cease to be controllable by elected officials, and that it will become arbitrary and tyrannical because the personal whims of low-level bureaucrats will no longer be adequately supervised from higher up. This span-of-control problem can be felt all up and down the line, but perhaps most acutely at the presidential level. Any department secretary, or even bureau chief, can employ devices such as management by objectives, program budgeting, cost/effectiveness analysis, and zero base budgeting to attempt to improve efficiency and coordination within the agency itself, where it may be presumed that there is a high degree of consistency among the agency's component programs and goals. For an active president, the problems of control are of a far different and more intractable character.

There is, first of all, a thorough-going ambiguity in the notion of presidential control of the bureaucracy. If it is assumed that departments and agencies have clear programmatic goals already, then presidential control is nothing more than the president carrying out the consitutional responsibility to see that the laws be executed. But presidential preferences may often be at odds with the procedures and goals built up over the years by the career civil servants within each department. The members of the Cabinet are perhaps not the president's natural enemies, as has sometimes been observed, but they certainly are not the president's natural allies.[10] Even political appointees come to defend their department's position against overly zealous White House coordination. So presidential control may be at odds with bureaucratic effectiveness to the extent that presidents try to force agencies to do something they do not want to do, and to press single-mindedly for political control might mean settling for a less efficient administrative apparatus.

The history of the modern activist presidency is one of organizational innovation designed to make the executive branch more manageable according to the preferences and style of each incumbent. The history begins in 1921, with the creation of the Bureau of the Budget and the unified executive budget. These for the first time gave the president a view of the overall executive enterprise, and were a beginning for presidential budgetary control. The Bureau of the Budget was moved into the newly created Executive Office of the President in 1939, and under Presidents Roosevelt and Truman the BOB took on the tasks of coordination and legislative clearance for the president's program.[11]

---

[10] The comment by Charles Dawes, first Director of the Bureau of the Budget, is quoted by Kermit Gordon, "Reflections on Spending," *Public Policy*, **XV**, (1966), p. 15.

[11] Richard E. Neustadt, "Presidency and Legislation: The Growth of Central Clearance," *American Political Science Review*, **48** (1954), pp. 641–71.

In the immediate postwar period, the Joint Chiefs of Staff, the Central Intelligence Agency, and the National Security Council were created (1947), and a series of interim military arrangements was given new status as the Department of Defense (1949). The NSC (located in the Executive Office of the President) along with the Defense Department, curtailed the traditional autonomy of the military services. Eisenhower's two terms saw regularizing of the White House staff and the creation of the Department of Health, Education and Welfare to replace the Federal Security Agency created by the same 1939 reorganization plan that produced the Executive Office.

The Planning Programming Budgeting System (PPBS) began in the Defense Department in 1961, and President Johnson mandated its extension to all domestic agencies in 1965. If we judge by complaints from the military, the introduction of PPBS with President Kennedy's blessing was clearly an attempt to increase central control. Domestic applications proved much more difficult and confusing, and although PPBS was also intended as an instrument of central control in the domestic sphere, it is questionable whether presidents have gained much from it.[12] Similarly, the Department of Housing and Urban Development (1965) and the Department of Transportation (1966) have been only imperfectly successful as instruments of central coordination for the diversity of programs in these areas.

The most far-reaching and ambitious efforts at executive centralization were made during the Nixon administration. In 1969, common regional boundaries and eight common regional centers were established for the Department of Labor, HEW, HUD, the Office of Economic Opportunity, and the Small Business Administration. The departments in each of the eight regions coordinated their policies through a regional council. In 1970, the Executive Office was reorganized into an Office of Management and Budget and a Domestic Council. The OMB took over the management responsibilities of the Bureau of the Budget, and the Domestic Council assumed policy making and evaluat-

---

[12] Allen Schick, "A Death in the Bureaucracy: The Demise of Federal PPB," *Public Administration Review*, **33** (1973), pp. 146–56.

ing duties. Paralleling the National Security Council, the Domestic Council included the secretaries from the domestic departments, meeting under the chairmanship of the vice president.

In 1971, President Nixon proposed a Federal Executive Service to replace the political appointees at the supergrade level in the civil service, a major reorganization of seven domestic departments into four, and a reorganization of the foreign assistance programs. All these proposals required legislative action, and Congress did not act favorably on any. Because of congressional unwillingness to disrupt legislative ties with the existing departmental structure, Nixon reorganized the White House staff in 1973 to achieve the same ends. This somewhat ad hoc arrangement placed five presidential assistants immediately below the president and elevated three Cabinet level secretaries to the position of White House counselor. The three counselors were given coordinating responsibilities similar to those of the Departments of Natural Resources, Human Resources, and Community Development proposed in 1971. The Secretary of the Treasury, already selected as one of the five presidential assistants, held responsibilities similar to those of the 1971 proposal for a Department of Economic Affairs. The Executive Office was further streamlined in 1973 by abolishing the Office of Emergency Preparedness, the Office of Science and Technology, and the National Aeronautics and Space Council.

President Ford continued the pattern of executive innovation. Within two weeks of taking office, he created an economic policy board drawing its members from the Cabinet and meeting to coordinate economic forecasting and advice. In the 50 years since the Bureau of the Budget began its work, significant improvements have been made in presidential control of the federal bureaucracy, yet every president has found those powers inadequate. The ambiguity in executive control surfaces here again; improving presidential control may increase the likelihood that a political commitment to respond to a social issue will be translated speedily into some kind of bureaucratic response, but excessive central executive control may diminish the effectiveness of the bureaucracy in carrying out both new tasks and existing responsibilities.

The danger of excessive centralism is not merely hypothetical. For instance, the frustration of the Nixon administration at the imperfections of presidential control led to extensive efforts to call to heel the independent regulatory agencies, supposedly responsible only to Congress.[13] Agencies in the executive departments complained of excessive interference from the Office of Management and Budget, and congressional investigators claimed to have found widespread use of political influence in federal hiring in at least two departments and three other major federal agencies during the Nixon administration.[14] These extraordinary, occasionally extralegal, efforts to impose presidential control are evidence of the basic weakness of central direction rather than signs of effective presidential management. And whether effective or not, they reveal a basic limitation in the use of bureaucracies to implement responses to social issues.

Social Experiments: The New Wave?

Many of the social issues that have concerned politicians in recent years have been new or recurring versions of some of society's most persistent problems. Poverty, health care, racial prejudice, unemployment, basic educational opportunity—there has been little need for sophisticated indicator systems to show the existence of trouble in these areas. For the most part, politicians have been looking for solutions rather than new problems. This need, and the inability of the societal monitoring approach to generate specific policy recommendations, led to a movement for social experimentation in the late 1960s and early 1970s.

An attractive feature of the social experimentation approach is its appeal to both liberals and conservatives. Liberals are optimistic that a carefully designed and implemented pilot project will show the effectiveness of a particular social intervention strategy; conservatives hope that the trial run will show the

---

[13] Wayne E. Green, "Feeling the Heat: Regulatory Agencies, In Theory Independent, Face Nixon Pressure," *Wall Street Journal,* July 21, 1970.

[14] "Improper Federal Hiring Reported in Nixon Years, *"Minneapolis Tribune,* October 11, 1974.

strategy's unworkability. Even if they are wary, liberals see the logic in putting their ideas to a practical test; even if they would prefer to see nothing at all in the way of government intervention, conservatives may be consoled by the opportunity to head off a full-scale program or at least to delay it for a few years. Disagreements surface again when the results are in and a judgment must be made: did the experiment work, or not?

Social experiments are proceeding all the time, of course. Even the routine application of the most commonly accepted social policies can constitute a social experiment if someone collects and analyzes the evidence from this viewpoint. Conscious experimentation, funded by government agencies for the explicit purpose of testing new social strategies was not common prior to the 1960s, however. Social scientists interested in evaluating social policies were forced to come in after the fact and attempt to reconstruct what had happened because they were not generally allowed to participate in the implementation decision—the "design" stage of the experiment. When the evaluators offered their conclusions, it was easy for the bureaucrats to push them aside. The program was not designed as an experiment, they could say, or the researchers collected the wrong data, or they did not really understand what the program was trying to do, and in any case their methods were faulty. Thus the unplanned experiment proved to be of little use in adding to government intelligence.[15]

Research in juvenile and adult corrections programs illustrates these difficulties with clarity. For decades, city, county, and state law enforcement agencies, courts, parole boards, and prison officials have engaged in haphazard experimentation in an effort to reduce recidivism—the repeating offender. Sometimes projects have been based on sociological theory, on other occasions they have been formed out of desperation, guesswork, public relations problems, or the personal philosophies of corrections officials. Researchers who have evaluated these experiments, including some who participated in designing them, have

---

[15] Alice M. Rivlin, *Systematic Thinking for Social Action,* Washington, Brookings, 1971, Chapters 4 and 5.

concluded that no form of correctional program really "corrects" the offender.[16] An inclination to recidivism is an individual peculiarity, or a phenomenon of social context, but it is probably beyond the reach of the correctional system. Indeed, the research findings often show perverse effects; that is, imprisoning offenders increases their chances of commiting another crime, keeping offenders locked up longer exacerbates the effects of imprisonment, using intensive forms of counseling and other behavior modification techniques may be worse than leaving offenders alone. Parolees are more often guilty of technical parole violations when they are watched closely than when supervision is lax.

Professional corrections officials have almost unanimously rejected or ignored the implications of this research. Costly programs using approaches demonstrated to have little or no beneficial effect continue in many prisons and parole systems because the corrections bureaucracies had no commitment to the research effort and were not forced, politically or otherwise, to pay any serious attention to the results.[17] Academic intelligence does not readily become governmental intelligence, especially when it threatens the beliefs and careers of government personnel. Where ineffective or detrimental programs have been terminated, the reason has usually been budgetary rather than programmatic. Corrections officials still favor extensive counseling, drop-in youth centers, remedial education and job training programs, halfway houses, or whatever their chosen device may be, but these have been let go in the face of tightening budgets and citizen complaints about the high cost of corrections.

Two critical elements lacking in the corrections field were careful researcher control of the experiments and official commitment to the experiments as information-gathering devices. Is experimentation more effective when these elements are pre-

---

[16] James Robison and Gerald Smith, "The Effectiveness of Correctional Programs," *Crime and Delinquency,* **17** (1971), pp. 67–80.

[17] David A. Ward and Gene G. Kassebaum, "On Biting the Hand That Feeds: Some Implications of Sociological Evaluations of Correctional Effectiveness," in Carol H. Weiss, ed., *Evaluating Action Programs,* Boston, Allyn and Bacon, Inc., 1972, pp. 300–10.

sent? Between 1967 and 1972 the Office of Economic Opportunity was involved in two major social experiments that offer perhaps the best evidence on the usefulness of government sponsorship of social experimentation.

Between 1967 and 1972, OEO designed, contracted for, conducted, and analyzed the results of an experiment in income maintenance.[18] The experiment, conducted in New Jersey and Pennsylvania, tested the effects on family income and work force participation of eight different negative income tax plans. It reached 1357 families in four cities and cost $8 million. Both its supporters and its detractors agree that the experiment showed several things: large-scale social experiments can be done; they are costly; they are complex and hard to do correctly.

There is less agreement about its substantive findings. Most observers agree that the work force effects of a negative income tax were shown to be small, but some say this was because most recipients were not given very high benefit levels or were not forced to submit to high tax rates. Others question whether the impact on work values of a hypothetical permanent national income guarantee plan can validly be inferred from a localized limited experiment. Some experimental results remain unexplained, casting doubt on the representativeness of the experimental sites and the participants. Finally, the state of New Jersey confounded part of the experiment by putting into effect in 1969 an AFDC-UP program that was more generous than two of the eight negative income tax plans being tested by OEO.

During the 1970–71 school year, OEO was also involved in funding an experiment in educational performance contracting.[19] Twenty school districts across the country were involved, with 20,000 students and seven contracting firms, at a total cost of $6 million. The object in this experiment was to see whether elementary school students, especially those from disadvantaged backgrounds, could be taught more effectively with sophisti-

---

[18] Joseph A. Pechman and P. Michael Timpane, eds., *Work Incentives and Income Guarantees,* Washington, Brookings, 1975.

[19] Edward M. Gramlich and Patricia P. Koshel, *Educational Performance Contracting,* Washington, Brookings, 1975.

cated educational technology and contracts rewarding the instructional firm for student advancement than with traditional methods. Again, the experiment itself proved to be more complicated than would have been thought at first, and the results proved more difficult to measure than most participants had anticipated. OEO had essentially no control over the teaching methods employed by the different contracting firms, so it was impossible to draw definite conclusions about the effectiveness of different teaching techniques versus the effectiveness of performance contracting itself. The usual questions about the representativeness of sites were raised, and the internal debates and lawsuits between OEO and the contractors after the experiment was terminated revealed widespread disagreement about the meaning of educational achievement.

Did these experiments contribute significantly to governmental intelligence? The income maintenance tests definitely allayed official fears about work force effects, especially in Congress. Indeed, critics worried that Congress might overreact to the experiment and pass a negative income tax plan disregarding all the other troublesome aspects of such a scheme. In any event, assurances that few people would stop working just because the government gave them some money did not provide the positive boost the Family Assistance Plan needed to get over the hurdles of Senate politics, but the experiment did affect attitudes.

Judging by its effect on local school district decisions, the performance contracting experiment was a spectacular success. The year following the experiment, only one of the 20 school districts continued some form of performance contracting, and virtually no school system now uses performance contracting of the type tested in 1970–71. Since local school districts were not committed in any way to accept or act on the results of the study, their ready acceptance of its results show its persuasiveness (although teacher opposition to performance contracting clouds this explanation somewhat). Yet OEO's role was really little more than that of funding agency. The lessons were learned not because OEO had insisted on a high-quality experiment, or because the authority of OEO stood behind the results, but because 20 school districts were given the financial incentive to try performance contracting at a critical point in the spread of this idea within educational circles. Indeed, the lasting contribution to government intelligence on educational technology may be unduly prejudicial to the approach tested in 1970. In simplified form, the results are "performance contracting doesn't work." In reality, all the study said, and that with considerable reservation about its generality, is "performance contracting isn't any better than traditional methods, but it isn't any worse either." Clarification of educational goals and improvements in educational technology may again make performance contracting a competitive approach.

"The Old Ways Are Good Enough"

Social indicators, if they exist, are most useful in setting the long-term governmental agenda. By anticipating problems, they allow politicians to observe their development and design a phased response or a cut-off at some critical point before the symptoms of the problem become unmanageable. For every three problems coming down the road toward you, as the saying goes, two will have fallen away by the time you must act. But you will still be in trouble if you didn't see the one that did get through. A good social monitoring system gives some kind of voice to otherwise unarticulated demands. Lacking advance warning, politicians are reduced to interpreting ambiguous cries for help and responding to them under the immediate pressures of the issue. Similarly, social experiments can provide valuable evidence of the workability of possible solutions. Yet the experiments with experimentation in recent years have had a depressing effect on this approach. Without a handy list of proved solutions, politicians are forced to live by their wits and the repertoire of pseudoresponses (catalogued in later chapters) familiar to observers of American politics.

The urban rioting of the 1960s, especially the Watts riots in 1965 and the Newark riots in 1967, demonstrated the limits of these "old ways" in extreme form. To begin with, there was no agreement that riots were veiled pleas for help, or if they were, that they were legitimate means of expression. There was no immediate authoritative explanation for the riots, and official resentment was as common a reaction as sympathy. After all, this was the administration that had declared a war on poverty, and initiated the Job Corps and the Model Cities program (ironically called Demonstration Cities at the time) as earnest of its intentions. Was black rioting purely random? Fomented by revolutionaries and criminal elements? A symptom of frustration? Or what? The National Advisory Commission on Civil Disorders (the Riot Commission), set up to answer these questions, could answer them only by reconstructing the social monitoring information that could have been gathered before the riots. This the Commission staff proceeded to do, but their results were not available for almost eight months.[20]

Meanwhile, a majority of white Americans and a near unanimity of big city police chiefs, not burdened by the Riot Commission's doubts, had called for a strong riot control response, and their resistance to "condoning the riots" prejudiced any attempt to understand the rioters' frustrations. When it appeared a year later, the commission's definition of the issue as white racism could not mollify this view,[21] so the poverty warriors in Washington lost a chance to underline the need for preventive aid to riot-prone areas because they were unprepared to urge such an issue definition when the riots occurred.

The lack of advance commitment to the report of a blue ribbon commission such as the Riot Commission is a serious shortcoming of this device, although it is perfectly understandable politically. If politicians are to be stuck with a possibly unpopular political view, they naturally want to be able to assess it and make the decision themselves. The Riot Commission report was not well received when its indictment of white racism was made public because politicians had not prepared themselves for this point of view. When asked point blank in public whether

---

[20] *Supplemental Studies for the National Advisory Commission on Civil Disorders,* Washington, Government Printing Office, 1968.

[21] *Report of the National Advisory Commission on Civil Disorders,* New York, Bantam Books, 1968, pp. 203–6.

they agreed with this assessment, many were not willing to go along, especially as they had reason to pride themselves on several years of concentrated attention to the problems of minorities and the core cities.

The report of the Commission on Obscenity and Pornography, created by Congress in 1967, met an even more spectacular fate when it was made public in September 1970. The Senate immediately held hearings on the report (it was an election year, after all), featuring prominently the minority spokesmen from the Commission. In mid-October, a resolution was brought to the Senate floor, sponsored by 50 Senators, stating that the Commission had not complied with the Congressional mandate, and that its findings and recommendations were not supported by the evidence available to the Commission. The resolution specifically rejected the Commission's conclusions that there is no connection between exposure to pornography and criminal behavior or moral deterioration, and went on to reject its recommendation that restrictive legislation applying to consenting adults be repealed.

The Senate resolution was duly passed on a 60 to 5 roll call vote, and the Commission's two years of work and several million dollars of expense were summarily laid to rest. Sometimes politicians can decide where they stand a lot more rapidly than ordinary mortals.[22]

In this instance, as in others where existing policy commitments seem to blow up in bureaucrats' faces, the ideal intelligence apparatus would be *both* program evaluation and social monitoring. Without social monitoring of some kind bureaucrats would be unable to see the disaster coming down the road; without program evaluation they might be unable to prove that their own efforts did not add to the fire. In either case, bureaucrats may lose their ability to influence the definition of the issue that is ultimately acted upon.

Do politicians refuse to look at developing social issues until

---

[22] For a criticism of the report, see Lane V. Sunderland, *Obscenity: The Court, The Congress and The President's Commission,* Washington, American Enterprise Institute for Public Policy Research, 1975.

they erupt as domestic policy crisis? They are certainly not ig-
norant of the techniques for assessing social problems and testing social intervention schemes—these have both been advocated and used with success. Nearly every agency does some
kind of social monitoring of its own, even if no common body of
social indicators has yet been assembled. Program evaluation is
also routine throughout much of the federal government, and
bureaucrats claim that evaluation studies *are* used, even though
they can rarely point to any dramatic effects directly traceable to
them.[23]

The problem lies, rather, in two related areas: government
capacity and political foresight. Social experiments, for example,
can be valuable when they demonstrate that a given technique is
workable or effective, but a really satisfying experiment usually
costs too much to use routinely. Further, the social experimentation approach pretends to offer isolated, absolute assessments of
the desirabiltiy of programs, and the lesson learned is often that
the payoff from a program, once it has been tested, is so small
that full operation is not justified. No matter that nothing better
is available or even under discussion.

In reality, this kind of advice is not very helpful for policy
makers. Their political problem is usually finding the one response consistent with budgetary constraints that offers the
greatest (relative) success and antagonizes the fewest people. So
the limits on government capacity may, in the end, be political in
nature rather than technical. The political element figures
strongly in the remaining chapters, which look first at the details
of the issue translation process and then evaluate various kinds
of policy response.

[23] Michael Q. Patton et al., *In Search of Impact: An Analysis of the Utilization of
Federal Health Evaluation Research,* Minneapolis, Minnesota Center for
Sociological Research, 1975.

4

How Issues Get on the Public Agenda

The next two chapters follow a social issue through the complete sequence of steps by which it is eventually resolved in some government program or authoritative statement of public policy. The description is idealized in the sense that some issues do not pass through the entire sequence successfully, but it will prove useful for later discussion of translation failure if the process is first described as an ideal model. Shortcomings can then be identified more readily when they occur in the real world of politics.

Social Problems

Social issues, and the issue translation process, begin with social problems, and these in turn begin with the perceptions and beliefs of citizens. A social problem may be defined as "a condition identified by significant groups within the population as a deviation from a social standard, or a breakdown of some important facet of social organization." It is, in short, a widely felt deficiency or disappointed expectation.[1] As expectations rise and fall, so too will the number of social conditions that appear to be

[1] Robert A. Dentler, *Major American Social Problems,* Chicago, Rand-McNally, 1967, p. 5.

problems. More complex, competent, and affluent societies, having more range for social disorder and more expectations that can fail, also have greater scope for social problems.

By definition, social problems occur in social contexts and involve large numbers of people, but their basis may just as well be individual as social. For instance, they may be individual problems such as a perceived lack of opportunity, or personal feelings of inadequacy and inferiority, and these problems may be shared by large numbers of people who recognize themselves as belonging to a distinct class or category. They may also be "inherently social," in that they can be traced directly to social interactions among classes of people. A sense of race or class unfairness, or class-related outrage at the illegal or antisocial behavior of others, would illustrate social problems of this second type.

Discrimination against women, and especially the implicit limitation of women to the roles of housewife and mother, may be seen to have both these features. Women actually occupying these roles may feel their inferior status as an individual burden and recognize that other women are, individually, in similar positions. More generally, women not confined to these roles may feel that they are opposing widely held social norms, accepted and passed on by a broad cross-section of society (including many women).

Many social problems in the United States are endemic, or at least remarkably resistant to solution. Problems under the general headings of war, poverty, and ethnic group relations fall into this category. Others are identified broadly by their location, either urban or rural. These are often legacies of spatial change in social and economic patterns, such as suburban sprawl, urbanization, rural depopulation. Individual deviant behavior, including crime, juvenile delinquency, and mental disorder, also seems likely to be a source of social problems as long as there are societies.

More than one specific problem from a single area may occupy a society concurrently. Black-white relationships have been the source of many specific problems in the past few decades, for instance, and these have coexisted with tensions of several kinds between whites and American Indians. Black and Indian "problems" resulted initially from growing expectations of better treatment on the part of blacks and native Americans themselves, and both groups have picked up allies from among the white majority.[2] Other observers, who do not take sides in these controversies directly, have simultaneously identified problems of social disorganization *within* these ethnic groups. The controversial debate over disintegration of the black family, and deteriorating conditions on Indian reservations, are instances of side problems perhaps caused or accelerated by the larger social forces in ethnic relations, but generally discussed separately. Where solutions have been sought, they have been separate solutions.

The Generation of Issues

The collection of social problems facing a particular society is not a static quantity, although many problems seem to persist for a long time and become bound up with the basic structure of social life. From time to time, specific manifestations of a basic social problem rise to the surface, gain widespread visibility, and may even be translated successfully into public policy, but the underlying problem still persists. One-time problems may also fade in significance without ever becoming translated into social issues and then into public policy. For example, some aspects of sex discrimination, such as access to education and career opportunities for women, have been or are being resolved without much direct governmental help, but at the same time feminists felt the necessity for an Equal Rights Amendment to the U.S. Constitution. Affirmative action programs are helpful, but they are rarely the underlying explanation for equal rights progress. They were mandated when women had already begun to break into traditionally male-dominated fields. These events are less

---

[2] Recent research is critical of the rising expectations hypothesis. See Abraham H. Miller, Louis H. Bolce, and Mark Halligan, "The J-Curve Theory and the Black Urban Riots," *American Political Science Review,* 71 (1977), pp. 964–82.

cause-and-effect, however, than they are common effects of a single cause, the women's movement. In other words, the emergence of equal rights as a *social* issue was the critical event.

Defined most briefly, a social issue is a social problem about which there is social disagreement over the solution. In public discussion we often seek a clear statement of "the issue," perhaps in the forlorn hope that we could begin to solve a problem if we could somehow isolate "the issue" from the welter of arguments pressing in from all sides. Often the precise meaning of the term "issue" is obscure, even though there may be substantial agreement on the issue itself. In the matter of amnesty for Vietnam draft resisters, for example, there was general agreement on what was "at issue"; that is, there was general agreement on the subject of discussion. Put simply, this was the postwar treatment of draft resisters. Commonly, what is "at issue" is a collection of valuables that will be endangered if a change of social policy is not made or a specific public action is not taken. It is, therefore, a real problem, with some sense of urgency motivating the search for a solution.

In the amnesty question a great many people expressed concern about amnesty because they had draft-resisting relatives living outside the United States. But these worries, in themselves, do not explain the sense of urgency that developed in 1974 as the Vietnam war officially came to an end. Urgency arose just then because the government had issued various statements signalling a willingness to discuss the policy. The resignation of President Nixon offered a timely opportunity to resolve the issue, and the new president found that he had a strong political incentive to adopt some form of amnesty program. "Binding up the nation's wounds" was President Ford's official rationale; providing cover for a pardon for Richard Nixon was on his secret agenda.[3] Amnesty therefore became a subject of renewed discussion owing to a mixture of public and governmental opportunity.

[3] W. Lance Bennett et al., "Deep and Surface Images in the Construction of Political Issues: The Case of Amnesty," *Quarterly Journal of Speech,* **62** (1976), pp. 110–26.

The somewhat unfocused amnesty debate did not produce a clear statement of "the issue" prior to President Ford's announcement in late 1974 of the administration's alternate service scheme. Because the Ford program became government policy by means of executive order, the detailed analysis and debate that most executive policy proposals usually receive did not occur. Once the Ford policy was in force, however, those members of the public still interested in discussing the issue reorganized themselves around a new definition: will the Ford plan work? Into this new (but substantially less controversial and less public) issue, those still involved read their own concerns. The Ford administration staked out a simple position—the plan was a positive answer to the question of workability. However, having a concrete plan to attack, critics then began to ask not about effectiveness, but about appropriateness: is it fair to impose such severe penalties on individuals with strong moral beliefs against the war? Is it fair to impose such high costs on the families of draft resisters?

"At issue," then, is a general problem area. "The issue" itself, as any one actor or group sees it, can usually be expressed as a question relating to one or more specific proposals for action. Will it work? Will it work better than what we now have? Will it do anything undesirable besides what it was designed to do?

Issue Publics

Social problems are recognized as such by substantial numbers of people, including many who are not directly affected by the problem, as the result of a process that is usually gradual and, for the most part, unconscious. In short, social problems (as perceived by society) are the product of natural social forces. No particular theory explains the emergence of social issues from problems so perceived, unless it is the simple notion of unplanned social communication, or social learning. From the great number of two-person social interactions, and from mass media sources, some few items of information are identified by people who receive them, and reinforced by other social communication, as significant social controversies. These are filed away, perhaps later to become the basis of opinion and action under the appropriate circumstances.[4]

In the case of the draft resisters, for instance, they and their immediate family and friends saw resistance as a symptom of a social problem from the beginning because the antiwar movement attempted to portray it in this light. Perception of the issue expanded rather quickly to nondraftee members of the antiwar movement, also, because the fate of draftees and draft resisters was highly salient to them. Considerably more time was needed to bring the problem to the attention of members of the public affected neither by antiwar sentiment nor draft resistance within their immediate social circle.

In the pregovernmental phase there is no official agency for sanctioning a single definition of a social problem. There will be a diversity of views, reflecting both differences in information (the extent to which a person is tied into the broader social communication network) and differences in values (divergent views of the question based on personal styles or the perceived individual impact of the problem). This whole process of social discussion is often described as "defining the issue," but the rarity of agreement on a single definition suggests that there is no necessity for agreement. An issue, that is to say a social problem with many definers and a multiplicity of definitions as an issue, may proceed to the next step without any of its ambiguities having been resolved. Perhaps the most accurate statement of what is happening is simply that "the issue is joined." The initial identifiers of the problem rephrase their views as an issue position—a statement of recommended action—and at least one other group of people reacts, or presents a differing issue position on its own.

Why is the issue joined? E. E. Schattschneider's classic analysis of political conflict[5] suggests two principles about conflict partic-

---

[4] A useful discussion of this process can be found in M. Brewster Smith, Jerome S. Bruner, and Robert W. White, *Opinions and Personality*, New York, Science Editions, 1964.

[5] E. E. Schattschneider, *The Semisovereign People*, New York, Holt, Rinehart and Winston, 1960, Chapter 1.

ipation: the "tremendous contagiousness" of conflict, and the strategic importance of the scope of conflict. In the first instance, conflicts are believed to attract unbidden spectators and participants; in the second, participants are advised to control the scope of a conflict to control its outcome.

Conflicts and "causes" are attractive to outsiders for several reasons. Most basically, they offer an opportunity for "pure" self-expression, or for expressing frustration with social events beyond individual control. When this is the case, outsiders join for essentially nonpolitical reasons. They probably do not estimate carefully the chances of success for their protest, because the rewards from involvement do not depend on success.

Second, conflicts may appear to be opportunities for successful demands for change. Here, the joiners believe that disagreement signals an unexpected expansion of the realm of feasible policy choices. Outsiders join because this unanticipated loosening of politics raises individual hopes for political change and brings previously dormant personal concerns into the open. There may also be something of a bandwagon effect. Here again, outsiders joining a conflict may not analyze their chances of success very carefully, but unlike the first group they do care about success. As Schattschneider suggests, they may therefore be particularly susceptible to manipulation by entrepreneurs for one side of the issue or the other.[6]

Finally, participation in a social conflict may be largely artifactual—the real attraction may be only spectatorship, much like sports watching, enhanced by mass media coverage of political events. The media make spectatorship possible, but the basic urge to watch comes from the spectators themselves.

The mass media are also partly implicated in the first listed reason, for it is only with mass media coverage of social and political happenings that large numbers of people are forced to confront unpleasant and frustrating realities beyond those they experience personally. Coverage of wars, riots, education and health policy problems and disputes, or the race and poverty burdens of others, *may* breed social sympathy. It may also con-

---

[6] Schattschneider, *The Semisovereign People,* Chapters 1 and 4.

tribute to frustration and a detached spectatorial attitude, because it allows vicarious participation in a much wider range of
events than even the most passionately committed social activist
could manage.

An unfortunate, but probably inevitable consequence of the
inflated "participation" rates for public questions in modern
societies is that policy makers can rarely judge the true extent of
serious concern concealed in mass attitudes. Collectively, the
American public is not without an opinion on almost any subject,
whether it is based on information or not, and whether or not it
implies any underlying stable basis of commitment. Americans
by and large are not heartless and unfeeling: if they hear of the
plight of some group other than their own (as they often will,
given the propensity of the mass media to treat news stories
from the point of view of "human interest" and entertainment
value) they will be duly sympathetic. Gallup pollsters measuring
public sentiment at about the same time will discover that a
relatively large proportion of the population has an opinion
about the plight of that group. But this opinion comes very close
to being politically irrelevant—and most politicians know that to
be the case—because the opinion is formed on virtually no information, reflects human sympathy rather than policy assessment of any kind, and is of so low an intensity that no political
action would be expected to come from it. Indeed, politicians
may feel that "opinions" of such a low intensity perhaps *should*
not be given much weight in the policy process.

To summarize what has been said so far, it appears that there
are at least two processes taking place in these early stages of
issue translation. The first is the joining of the issue, and the
second is the process by which issue publics emerge. The issue is
joined by groups fearing the consequences of the initial statement of the problem, should that statement result in substantial
governmental response, or by groups, probably led by entrepreneurs with a "professional" interest in expressing their group's
viewpoint, that cannot keep silent in the face of what they feel is
a misstatement of the problem.

Issue publics emerge either as separate mass followings of
joiners for each of the separately stated issue positions—people

seeking an expressive outlet, or feeling that effective change may be enhanced by their support for the stated problem—or as sidetakers, in the manner of Schattschneider's crowd, seeing a conflict and feeling drawn to sympathize with one side or the other. The extent of side-taking depends on the emergence of a conflict; because distinct issue positions can be expressed by groups acting on their own rather than in direct oppostion to each other, the conflict may not immediately attract large issue publics. The chance occurrence of mass media coverage, or the calculated efforts of group leaders to seek wider publicity, will be important in expanding the conflict to masses of bystanders.

The various groups of participants in social issue generation are sometimes described as different levels of public. Cobb and Elder, in their study of agenda building, distinguish "the public of a group" from "an attention group."[7] A group's public includes those people identifying with the group and drawn into an emerging social issue by this identification. An attention group encompasses everyone concerned about an issue for its own sake; they are drawn to an emerging conflict because they care about the issue itself. Beyond these "publics" immediately involved with an issue, there is *the* attentive public—that small fraction of the population that pays regular attention to social issues as an aspect of good citizenship—and then the general public, whose involvement with politics tends to be superficial and disconnected. Using the amnesty example again, we can identify draft resisters themselves as "the group," members of their immediate social circle as their public, and people concerned about the war—whether opposed or supporting—as the attention group for the emerging amnesty issue. The attentive and general publics, by these definitions, would be identical to the attentive and general publics for all other issues.

Regardless of the terminology used, however, the important point is that people become involved to different degrees and for different reasons, and these differences will affect the history of an issue. In the absence of overt conflict or special efforts

---

[7] Roger W. Cobb and Charles D. Elder, *Participation in American Politics: The Dynamics of Agenda Building,* Boston, Allyn and Bacon, 1972, pp. 104–11.

to publicize an issue, some issue publics (a term generally including "publics of groups" and "attention groups") may not emerge until a problem has been taken up by government agencies. They will not become aroused until the threat posed by unfavorable official action has been made real to them. The late emergence of a potential issue public at the very least complicates and slows the translation process because it forces a redefinition of the issue midway through its career. Coming in late is usually not an advantage, however, because the "mutual adjustments" among partisans already involved will be difficult for the latecomers to overturn.[8]

The importance of being in at the beginning is nicely demonstrated by the early history of the War on Poverty, during the Kennedy and Johnson administrations.[9] In this instance a governmental strategy was selected almost entirely within the executive branch, although certainly informed by the public's attitudes on poverty. One set of policy advisers had been working in relative obscurity since 1961, formulating their own approach which was then adopted wholeheartedly and with little question by President Johnson for his own political purposes. Working from the President's Committee on Juvenile Delinquency and the Ford Foundation's Gray Areas project, and drawing theoretical justification from friendly social scientists, this group needed only presidential commitment to define the poverty issue and implement a solution at one stroke.

What Is on the Public Agenda?

In the Vietnam amnesty issue, as in most other areas of American social policy, public concern rose to a peak and then diminished again, to be replaced in the public mind by the next most interesting event or incipient issue. The suggestion of an

[8] Charles E. Lindblom, *The Intelligence of Democracy*, New York, The Free Press, 1965, pp. 217–20.

[9] For the intellectual development, see Peter Marris and Martin Rein, *Dilemmas of Social Reform*, New York, Atherton Press, 1967. For politics, see Richard Blumenthal, "Antipoverty and the Community Action Program," in Allan P. Sindler, ed., *American Political Institutions and Public Policy*, Boston, Little, Brown and Company, 1969.

agenda of public issues is not hard to find in this typical pattern of issue dynamics, even if the agenda is not written down or formalized in any way. The agenda has a definite existence as that set of issues on which the public currently believes action must be taken. A public agenda, in this view, is an aggregate of the individual agendas of everyone in the society.

There are several reasons for the importance of the agenda concept. First, since American politics is a representative democracy (or system of limited participation) rather than a direct one, it cannot be guaranteed that all potential issues (all social problems) will automatically come up for public consideration. The action of constructing a public agenda will weed out idiosyncratic concerns and emphasize those that have been cited by large numbers of people.

Second, the existence of a public agenda, if it contains only a few items, simplifies the problems associated with choosing among them and helps professional politicians apportion their time among issues. Granted, public agendas do not define specific priorities or state time limits or urgency factors in any direct way, but by showing that there are always other issues waiting to be dealt with, they vividly suggest the desirability of prompt response to the issue temporarily at the top of the list.

When it can be said to exist, a public agenda, together with official agendas, constitute the main stages of the translation process through which parties and interest groups must move their chosen issues if they seek to resolve them through governmental action. A brief picture of the issue translation process can be gained by looking at these two types of agenda and how issues move onto them and off again.

The Polls and the Public Agenda

So far, we have assumed that there is a workable way to identify a public agenda. What method should we use to do this? How stable are the agenda's contents? Do they relate logically to the rise and fall of real world political circumstances? If the public agenda does encompass privately held agendas, it may reflect only the public's divergent points of view, and thereby be so

Table 1

Consensus on the Most Important Problem Facing the Country, 1968 to 1975

Number of Problems Rated "Most Important"	By 10% or More of Sample	By 20% or More of Sample
1	2 polls	8 polls
2	4	12
3	9	0
4	2	0
5	1	0
6	1	0
7	1	0
8 or more	0	0
	20 polls	20 polls

Source: Gallup Opinion Index, relevant issues.

fragmented as to offer no useful guidance on the public's concerns; but it may instead reflect a surprising degree of consensus among members of the public on the major issues of the day.

The easiest way to measure the content of the public agenda is to use the periodic Gallup opinion soundings. For many years, the Gallup organization has asked national population samples some form of the question, "What do you think is the most important problem facing this country today?" The responses[10] give an estimate of what is on the public agenda, especially if they are examined over a period of several years to see patterns of change and to estimate the extent of unexplainable variance, or measurement error, in the answers given to this question.

During the seven-year period from mid-1968 to mid-1975, roughly the period included in the listing of 47 congressional issues in chapter 2, Gallup asked the "most important problem" question 20 times. Over the seven-year period, a total of 12 issue areas were cited at least once by 10% of the sample or more, as

[10] Before 1972, see George H. Gallup, *The Gallup Poll,* New York, Random House, 1972. Subsequently, see the *Gallup Opinion Index.*

the most important problem facing the country. If the somewhat arbitrary figure of 10% is taken as a reasonable threshhold, building in a safety margin to eliminate sporadic issues and minor inconsistencies in reporting of results, the Gallup evidence suggests that the public's perception encompasses relatively few major problem areas. Further, as Table 1 shows, the number of issues plaguing the country at any one time is even smaller—typically about three, when it could easily have been seven or eight. Another way to describe the results is to say that the extent of social consensus on the most important problem is often quite high, there being typically one high scoring problem with the others receiving substantially lower scores.

The content of the issues mentioned to the Gallup pollsters makes intuitive sense in comparison with the dominant focus of politics of the time also, suggesting that the poll results really do represent a public agenda. Vietnam, the highest scorer from 1968 on into 1971, slowly declined in importance, finally dropping from view in mid-1973. Crime, also a big issue in 1968, the year the Omnibus Crime Control and Safe Streets Act was passed, declined thereafter to a level generally below 10% of the respondents. Youth protest enjoyed a brief flurry associated with the spring 1970 demonstrations against the Cambodia incursion, and the energy crisis topped the list in the winter of 1973–74, with the oil embargo and fuel shortages. The cost of living increased in significance over the whole period, being top problem from 1973 on except when (once) overshadowed by energy shortages. Unemployment was important in 1973 and again in 1975, but never listed as the most prominent concern.

For several areas the poll results show some interesting patterns. Pollution was not listed as the most important problem by more than 14% of the poll respondents at any time in the seven-year period, and in 1974 and 1975 it dropped too low to be recorded separately at all. Similarly, race relations, an important issue in the 1960s, dropped to 16% or less from 1968 on, and disappeared entirely in 1974 and 1975. Neither Watergate nor trust in government questions scored highly—never as much as 20%—although they both responded to the Watergate investigation and impeachment hearings in 1973 and 1974.

Public Worries and Opportunity Agendas

It is hard to know exactly how someone might decide to answer the "most important problem" question—one might suspect, for instance, that many respondents would simply mention the first acceptable answer that occurred to them in order to get the nice Gallup lady off their doorstep. Unfortunately, the argument here is circular. People mention what they have been reading in the newpapers and seeing on television, but the news media decide what to report on the basis of what the public wants to hear about. To the degree that this is true, it does not help us understand the significance of the public agenda.

Fortunately, two related questions asked by the Gallup organization help to pinpoint the nature of public concerns. In October 1967, a sample was asked, "What is the most urgent problem facing you and your family today?" This was followed in November by the standard "most important problem" question. Sixty percent of the first sample listed the cost of living as their most urgent problem, 8% listed health, 5% Vietnam, 4% civil rights, and 3% unemployment. In the second sample, 50% listed Vietnam, 21% civil rights, only 16% cost of living, and the other problem areas were too infrequently mentioned to be coded separately. Obviously the American public does distinguish between personal problems and national policy concerns. It does not automatically transfer family difficulties to the national arena, and it is concerned about national issues that apparently have little personal impact on most respondents. The results of this comparison make the American public look at least mildly rational in its choice of issues.

The second comparison question, "Which three of these (listed) national problems would you like to see the Government devote most of its attention to in the next year or two?" was asked a sample in early May 1970, and the standard problems question was asked later the same month. Table 2 compares the results. Since the listed problems dealt only with domestic priorities and several of the spontaneously mentioned problems were international in scope, the fit cannot be expected to be perfect. Nevertheless, where similar issues are found in both samples, their rankings are quite different. Pollution ranks

Table 2

The "Opportunity Agenda" and the "Index of Public Worries," May 1970

| Opportunity Area | Frequency of Mentions: | | Public Worry |
	Rank	Rank	
Crime	1	5	Juvenile delinquency, crime and lawlessness, drug addiction
Pollution	2	—	
Education	3	—	
Poverty	4	—	
Disease	5	—	
Housing and slums	6	—	
Race Discrimination	7½	3	Racial strife, polarization of American people
Unemployment	7½	?(6	High cost of living)
Highway safety	9	—	
"Beautifying America"	10	—	
not asked	—	1	Campus unrest
not asked	—	2	Vietnam war
not asked	—	4	Other international problems

Source: see text.

surprisingly high in the first survey considering that it had been rarely volunteered during any of the 1968–75 period. Crime, the front-runner in the first survey, was mentioned almost dead last of the volunteered issues.

One significant distinction between the two surveys is the presence of second and third choices in the first and not (barring voluntary multiple responses) in the second. Pollution problems, it would appear, had been running a strong second or third, but rarely first on anyone's list; consequently pollution was hardly ever identified as the number one national problem. The real distinction, however, is that the listed items are opportunity questions while the most important problem is a question of immediate action. In the listed items, respondents are being told, in effect, "Assume that the opportunity existed over the next year or two to move ahead in several of these areas. Where would you like to see some progress made?" The opportunity assumption is critical, and it undoubtedly colors the nature of the public's responses.

In contrast, the items on the supposed public agenda derived from volunteered problem mentions are so mercurial in large part because they are not clearly articulated policy preferences, but merely worries or problems about which there is no agreement on what should be done. One worry may easily displace another and absorb the public's "capacity for worrying," in contrast with a definite decision to do something, which ceases to be a significant cause for worry once the decision has been made. It is possible, then, for governmental action to put to rest the most important problem identified at any one time by the public, but it could also be the case that these problems solve themselves before governmental action has had a chance to make much of an impact on them.

Which of these two kinds of questions identifies what is really on the public agenda? In fact neither does, because each has its shortcomings, but each goes part way. The answer lies in a comparison with institutional agendas. These are made by and for government institutions or government officals and built around a commitment to action. Institutional agendas are devices for scheduling decisions and actions, and because they are made by the same people who will then carry out the stated actions, they imply a commitment of institutional resources to the task of following through. If this model applied to public agendas, it would mean that politicians would respond to the issues on the public agenda because they felt forced to do so. They might not feel entirely confident of their ability to respond effectively, but respond they would because to do so (even unsuccessfully) would be more important politically than to fail to respond (even for all the best reasons).

The relatively short-lived items identified as the most important problems do meet the action-forcing requirements of the agenda notion, but not because they have been duly enrolled on an agenda. The public agenda is not an agenda *for* the public—it does not list public commitments to act, but is merely a set of public ideas about the appropriate content of the government's agenda. It is, as James E. Anderson observes, essentially a discussion agenda.[11] Politicians feel compelled to act on these items only to the extent that they can see, as each "most important problem" rises to prominence, that a particular coalition of political forces wants them to act. While politicians can often count on public indulgence, and even support, for governmental responses made under the gun in this fashion, political difficulties in identifying appropriate policies under public pressure often tempt politicians into symbolic responses when they cannot find real ones. It may be close to the mark to suggest that this kind of public agenda is really just an agenda for political speechwriters—it identifies for them the subjects on which politicians should be showing their concern, even if they are unprepared to go further in concrete response.

The opportunity agenda appears to reflect long-term issues of public concern better than the "index of current public worries" produced by the most important problem question, and the issues on the opportunity agenda are more stable. Unfortunately, they lack specificity even to the minimal extent that it is found in current public worries. As with the current worries list, the items on the opportunity agenda are not backed by anyone's commitment to act, and it is doubtful whether the public at large feels committed to support actions taken by officials with regard to issues supposedly on this public agenda. Politicians may be able to get along more comfortably with these issues because they have no action-forcing element. The public may be pleased if some action is taken on one or another of these priorities, but it will not usually be displeased if action is *not* taken, because there is really no way to identify the missed opportunities for which politicians can be blamed. Perhaps the best kind of political response to these issues is to treat them as priority items in routine policy making decisions such as budgetary allocations, where

[11] James E. Anderson, *Public Policy-Making*, New York, Praeger Publishers, 1975, p. 59. See also Anthony Downs; "Up and Down with Ecology—the 'Issue-attention cycle;" *The Public Interest*, **28** (Summer 1972), pp. 38–50.

government agencies can chip away at them over a period of years. At the same time, though, politicians should not expect great political reward for taking this approach, because the routine decisions that produce incremental results lack the drama and the hold on public attention exerted (if briefly) by the most important problems.

In summary, the so-called public agenda contains a few items of high importance for which political action (or action of some other kind) is actively sought, and a longer, more stable list of endemic problems for which some long-term response would be welcomed, but not required politically by any specific deadline date. Both the short and the long lists are distressingly vague about what the public really wants, and both are lacking in usable evidence on the intensity of feeling behind each issue. The public agenda is not the product of a single, unified public either. There are, rather, many publics, each with its own priorities. Even on a single issue there may be identifiable and separable (politically separable—differing in class, role, or geography) issue publics, each contributing part of the total. Politicians will disaggregate the issues on the agenda to respond to them, but the public at large may still be helped to understand its own mind(s) better through the efforts of pollsters to identify a public agenda.

5

How Issues are Processed in Government

Official Agendas

For those issues on the "index of current public worries," getting on a governmental agenda is the next significant event in a successful response pattern. Those issues on the public's "opportunity agenda" need not be placed on a government agenda, however, because they are already routine matters for government action. National defense, social services, maintenance of public order, and many others are traditional areas where the governmental role cannot be questioned. Although controversy may occur in any of these "endemic" policy areas at any time, routine bureaucratic decisions will be made in each of them regularly, and legislative decisions about funding levels will be made at least annually. Because policy decisions in these areas *are* made routinely, it is difficult to tell when an issue in any one of them is on the official agenda. The regular occasions for decision provide readymade opportunities to raise nonroutine questions without first having to persuade the public at large that such questions are worth pursuing. Thus the presidential moratorium on further commitments under the federal public housing program, imposed in 1973, was a device to force consideration of the program's deficiencies. Under this pressure, Congress responded in 1974 with a major restructuring of the public housing effort.

Official agendas are important for several reasons, even if it is sometimes difficult to tell whether an issue is on one or not. They are important because, unlike public agendas, they are commitments to action. When an issue has reached an official agenda, there is a good chance that it will be resolved because there is such a commitment and because politicians would not usually have allowed an issue onto an official agenda they controlled unless they felt they could respond satisfactorily.

Second, official agendas signal the relevant issue publics and issue entrepreneurs that action is imminent, and they indicate where action will take place. Indeed, official agenda setting may in some cases precede public agenda setting. This is likely to happen when reforms are initiated from within, as in the public housing example above. It may also happen when governmental receptiveness to a perennial issue pushes it forward on the public's opportunity agenda. Examples of this second mechanism—the War on Poverty in particular—are examined below, after which we return to governmental agendas themselves.

Issue Entrepreneurs

Most citizens are not political professionals. Their involvement, even for issues that concern them a great deal, is limited and sporadic. Similarly, with interest groups, typically a small number of full-time staff direct all the group's official actions, and the mass membership contributes only numbers and financial support. Social issues rarely emerge spontaneously from the unguided actions of large masses of people. They are generated sometimes by accidents of timing, but usually by conscious effort; sometimes unknowingly or unintentionally, but usually by people with issue generation as their specific goal. Along the line from issue generation to governmental response and issue resolution, there must be a number of critical people who facilitate movement in the issue translation process. Though their actions would not be sufficient to bring off the whole enterprise by themselves, these "issue entrepreneurs" are necessary parts of the process.[1]

Because issue entrepreneurs operate at several points in the overall issue translation process, there is no single best place to observe and describe them. This section will look over the shoulders of these distinctive political actors as they perform two critical roles, that of issue generator and issue broker. Sometimes the two roles may be filled by the same person, but in every instance the issue entrepreneur acts for the benefit of others and makes a livelihood by bringing about accommodations between citizen groups and public officials.

What is the role of issue generator—what exactly does one do? Individual citizens can generate issues, but most issues in the United States are given their major boost these days by politicians, interest groups, reporters for mass communications media, and others with regular or semiprofessional connections with political and governmental life. The critical act in generating an issue seems to be that of bringing it to the attention of large numbers of people who are already conscious of a shared interest, or who discover a shared interest as a result of becoming aware of the potential issue at about the same time. It will be useful to look separately at governmental and "private" initiators to see how they each affect the generation of issues.

Governmental officials play two roles in issue generation. They may, in the first place, publicize the potentially disastrous consequences of some government policy, or blow the whistle on a government scandal. Since the usual assumption about government officials is that they are bound to existing policies by links of bureaucratic loyalty and career-seeking, when they do break ranks and criticize existing policies (assuming there is reason to believe they know something about them), their statements are often highly regarded.

---

[1] The model for the issue entrepreneur can be found in C. Wright Mills, *White Collar,* New York, Oxford University Press, 1956, pp. 91–100. See also Robert H. Salisbury, "An Exchange Theory of Interest Groups," *Midwest Journal of Political Science,* **13** (1969), pp. 1–32.

For the same reasons that such statements are credible, however, they are also infrequent. They are often delivered by retiring or fired employees, and pose more of a temporary embarrassment than a serious challenge to policy makers. "Blasts" from employees forced out of government service are usually somewhat suspect because they are often tinged with personal bitterness, and may be thought to stem from personal antagonisms or even incompetence on the part of the fired employee. Unless the criticism can be supported with facts that speak with inherent authority, the case of the departing employee must be taken up by someone else, like a newspaper's investigative reporter, before much will come of it. This is true also because most departing employees do not follow up on their initial criticisms. They have more important things to do, such as finding a new job, and they do not often find the time to consider a possibly quixotic campaign against policies with which they were formerly involved.[2]

Three instances of political resignations, drawn from the more important few out of the large number that occur all the time, may show the problems in resigning effectively. In 1970, former Alaska Governor Walter Hickel resigned his position as Secretary of the Interior in the Nixon Cabinet. Although there were differences between Hickel and the White House over conservation policy questions, the main complaints Hickel raised were that he had been denied access to President Nixon and forced to work through presidential assistants Haldeman and Erlichmann. These complaints were real enough, but they obscured any substantive impact the resignation may have had. Few people outside government circles were interested in these internal bureaucratic difficulties, and they only made Hickel appear personally at fault.

In 1973, Attorney General Elliot Richardson resigned and Deputy Attorney General William Ruckelshaus was fired by President Nixon because both refused to fire the Watergate spe-

---

[2] For a rare example of an employee who did follow up his dismissal, see Leon E. Panetta and Peter Gall, *Bring Us Together: The Nixon Team and the Civil Rights Retreat,* Philadelphia, J. B. Lippincott Co., 1971.

cial prosecutor Archibald Cox. In this instance the circumstances of the case were clear to the news media and the
public because the White House and Cox had already fallen out
earlier over Cox's efforts to obtain White House tapes. Still,
President Nixon managed to present the issue as one of defiance
of presidential executive authority, thus partially defusing the
consequences of the firing.

A final example is the resignation of John T. Dunlop as Secretary of Labor in 1976. Dunlop was forced to choose between his
presidential and union loyalties when President Ford changed
his commitment to sign a bill allowing common-site picketing.
The resignation was decidedly anticlimactic, however, causing
much less stir than the initial Ford decision to veto the common-
site picketing bill. In any case Dunlop had held various labor-
related posts for a long time, for anyone brought into the government from the outside, and his departure was not entirely
unexpected.

Stimulating Issues

An important way for government officials to influence the generation of social issues is by appearing open to questions that
may previously have been relegated to a "nonissue" status. Receptiveness at the right time may be critical for the subsequent
progress of an issue even though government officials have not
themselves generated it. For instance, the declaration of a War
on Poverty by President Lyndon Johnson did a great deal to
influence congressional attitudes toward antipoverty programs,
and it encouraged interest groups and social welfare professionals to come forward with their solutions, so that the issue was
joined from a great diversity of viewpoints.

The War on Poverty is an early example of a pro-
gram-generating process eventually developed to a high degree
in the Johnson administration. Johnson felt that the government's main requirement at the time was good ideas, and to this
end he built an elaborate system of screening and program

choice.[3] Presidential assistant Joseph Califano and his aides were dispatched on yearly tours of university campuses and other likely idea centers. Their gleanings were reported to a high-level screening committee in the executive branch, and the proposals this committee recommended for further study were given to a secret task force. These bodies, made up separately for each major policy area, comprised representatives from the various functional groups likely to be involved with that policy. Each task force reported secretly to the president, and neither membership nor recommendations was ever acknowledged publicly.

The Johnson task forces—there were at least 50 of them— served well to bypass entrenched bureaucratic interests and gather policy ideas new to the administration. Their secret status freed task force members from external political influences and spared the administration the embarrassment of turning down policy recommendations. At the same time, however, the task forces did not actually invent any new ideas, and their suggestions ultimately had to be acceptable to existing government agencies.

Writing from a White House perspective, Thomas E. Cronin concluded that presidential commitment to new program ideas could not be expected unless the ideas were logical extensions of previous efforts, they had been incubated among the relevant professional and congressional constituency groups, and they were likely to serve the president's political needs.[4] In similar fashion, Harold Wolman reports that the 1968 housing proposals of the Johnson administration emerged from a process of institutional compromise involving at least nine distinct bureaucratic interests.[5] The task force device created to bypass the inertia of the federal bureaucracy had itself become bureaucratized and cumbersome.

---

[3] Norman C. Thomas and Harold L. Wolman, "The Presidency and Policy Formulation: The use of Task Forces," *Public Administration Review,* **29** (1969), pp. 459–71.

[4] Thomas E. Cronin, *The State of the Presidency,* Boston, Little, Brown and Company, 1975, p. 241.

[5] Harold Wolman, *The Politics of Federal Housing,* New York, Dodd, Mead and Company, 1971, p. 101.

What does an active presidency really contribute to the generation of social issues? At the least it will encourage discussion outside government circles. Task forces and executive commissions, with their direct representation of functional constituency groups, have been used to exert pressure on these groups to support governmental initiatives and, more generally, to mobilize public opinion support for the administration.[6]

But none of this creates truly new proposals. Lawrence Chamberlain's conclusions, now more than 30 years old, still seem correct. Studying the New Deal, another notable period of executive activism, Chamberlain tabulated a shift from congressional dominance to executive dominance. But the administration bills that eventually became law in the Roosevelt period had, in nearly every case, been prefigured by bills introduced and discussed in Congress some years before.[7] The real significance of this fact is simply that the ultimate source of legislative proposals is outside government altogether. The role of the executive, by no means a trivial one, is to put proposals otherwise destined to languish in Congress high on the agenda for prompt action. The prominence given to a proposal by the executive mobilizes forces inside and outside government and—often—brings together a coalition strong enough to insure passage when it would not otherwise have occurred.

The Entrepreneur as Inside-Dopester

The resource most commonly claimed by issue brokers who are not themselves part of the government apparatus is institutional access. They are "inside-dopesters"—they claim to know whom to talk to, and how to get things done. Thus they adopt issues when at least one side has already crystallized its position to some degree, where feasible responses exist, and where those responses can be sought with some chance of success from those institutions to which the broker has access.

[6] Wolman, *The Politics of Federal Housing,* pp. 90–2.
[7] Lawrence H. Chamberlain, "The President, Congress, and Legislation," *Political Science Quarterly,* **61** (1946), pp. 42–60.

The issue translation process, especially the problem of admitting a particular definition of an issue to an official agenda, usually requires entrepreneurs both inside and outside of government. In policy areas with a substantial history of government involvement, the insiders and the inside-dopesters typically work together on matters of strategy. For their part, the insiders must know the details of the policy making apparatus. They must be prepared to bring together the needed staff assistance to carry out research on a crash basis, draft and redraft legislative proposals, coordinate informational and lobbying campaigns within governmental circles, and, where necessary, lobby directly with higher executive authority.

When an issue has already been placed on an official agenda, the momentum of the issue translation process is regulated by personnel on the governmental side, and sympathetic outside groups must adjust their schedules and strategies to what is happening inside government. They have the difficult task of maintaining the interest of their membership, and readying them for a last-minute grassroots pressure campaign if one is needed. The constant flow of newsletters and legislative alerts must be kept up, the office must be staffed, research must be done, contacts must be renewed constantly with executive and legislative staff members, and suspicious elements of the membership must be persuaded that their interests are not being sold down the river in response to dictates from "higher up."

Social issues attract a number of interest groups when the point of decision on a specific set of policy proposals is reached, and the effort of organizing and coordinating the individual efforts of all these groups is considerable. The coordination problem is often given to a "peak association," a skeleton structure whose members are other interest groups and whose funding and staff are lent from the member groups. Ideally, liaison is carried out through this peak association and strategy is planned between it and sympathetic government representatives, although each member group will also try to secure direct access to governmental channels to show its membership that it, too, has clout in the legislature.

Where the key to successful governmental response is persuading the legislature to accept a plan sponsored by the executive branch, entrepreneurs in the executive branch may take the initiative, calling together the "national association for this" and the "coordinating committee for that," and hammering out an acceptable plan with these peak associations and their members.

Many of these elements of issue entrepreneurship are well illustrated by the coalition-building that preceded passage of the Elementary and Secondary Education Act of 1965, the first general aid to education measure ever passed.[8] Federal aid to education had been on official agendas sporadically for more than a decade, and public opinion majorities had supported it for longer than that, but proposals had always foundered on the church-state question, aid to segregated schools, or the old bugaboo of federal control. The 1964 elections, returning large numbers of liberal Democrats to Congress, offered the possibility that an aid bill could be passed if it found the right formula.

Over the years, the various groups concerned with aid to education had developed a substantial understanding of the issue and of each other's positions. Loose cooperative arrangements had existed in the past, both among supporters and opponents, and these groups were ready to go again as soon as a proposal was brought forward from the White House. If passage of the aid bill had been up to them, even with the new and heavily Democratic Congress, the bill would not have passed because the groups could not among themselves offer any new approaches to break the deadlock that aid bills had always encountered in the past. The new element in this case was Francis Keppel, the Commissioner of Education. Frustrated congressional Democrats had given the job of finding a workable compromise to the Johnson administration, and Johnson in turn passed the job on to Keppel.

During 1964 Keppel maintained contact with the various education and church groups, working with them to find areas of agreement and formulas for papering over disagreement. The master stroke was an executive drafted proposal to redefine the

[8] Eugene Eidenberg and Roy D. Morey, *An Act of Congress*, New York, W. W. Norton, 1969.

issue as aid to underprivileged children rather than assistance for poor school districts. When the bill reached Congress, the interest groups had little to do other than mobilize their local auxiliaries to pressure Congressmen to keep the bill intact, so tightly had the executive strategy been worked out. Even the National Education Association, the major interest group in the education field, was pulled back into line by the realization that an aid bill would be passed whether the NEA supported it or not.

This example shows how the nature of issue resolutions reflects the nature of political interests. As issues become more technical and interests more effectively organized, solutions require increasing degrees of negotiation and balance to be successful. Mere pressure or vote power may no longer suffice. For such work, skilled entrepreneurs are much in demand.

Operational Agendas

Every government body has an agenda setting device of some kind, but sometimes care is needed to find the operational agendas—those that really indicate which questions will receive constructive attention during a given time period. There is no problem for courts, especially appellate courts such as the Supreme Court and its parallels at the state level. Their dockets fill up quickly, largely beyond court control, and major cases may be scheduled as much as a year in advance. There will still be room for matters such as injunctive relief, where time is of the essence, but in these cases the need to act follows so shortly upon emergence of the issue that orderly agenda setting is not possible anyway.

Legislative agendas are found at several points in the legislative process. Every bill introduced during the session is referred to a committee, so the complete list of all introduced bills constitutes some kind of agenda. Of course, committees are not answerable to anyone for their legislative conduct, and they do not usually report on bills unless favorably. A bill not acted upon in committee may have been pigeonholed by the chairman, tentatively assigned to another session, passed over in favor of a more comprehensive bill, or partially incorporated in subsequent committee action. All bills reported out, or all bills on which hearings were held, might be a more realistic agenda, because committees have cared enough about those bills to expend some measurable effort in hearings or report writing.

Items reported favorably from committee may remain on a legislative calendar, awaiting final action, until the end of the two-year legislative term. Or they may be brought up and enacted immediately, as is the case with privileged business such as appropriations bills in the U.S. House of Representatives. Thus legislative calendars afford no sense of priority among items on the legislative agenda. Important measures may be delayed for executive input or extended hearings and markup, while routine items may be reported promptly at the beginning of a session and then languish on the calendar for lack of a sense of legislative urgency. Legislative agendas do not extend beyond the next election, but individual members and committee staff may sometimes sketch out a program of hearings and research over a several year period. Occasionally major items in the presidential or party program may be defeated or held over from one Congress to the next, and their sponsors will attempt to reintroduce these measures with bill numbers H.R.1 and S.1 to symbolize their importance, but this device does not guarantee them any special treatment.

Executive agendas are partially revealed in special messages, legislative proposals, State of the Union and State of the State addresses; but priority shifts and administrative reorganizations within existing programs are not always made public before they occur. The executive agenda has some of the ambiguity of the public agenda, also, in requiring positive actions by other governmental agencies, and therefore being an agenda for others as much as an agenda for executive action. It is not unknown for assertive chief executives, especially when faced with a legislative majority of the opposing party, to puff out their list of "must" legislation with an unreasonably large number of proposals, and then to use some as bargaining chips to aid the passage of others. When this is done, it is impossible to know which of the proposals was really on the agenda, because that decision is always subject to revision as executive bargaining strategies change during the course of the legislative session.

Conflicting Offical Agendas

The problem of ambiguous agendas always occurs when several governmental agencies must act in concert to complete the response to a social issue. In every instance, the presence of an issue on the agenda of one agency (say Congress) implies commitments to favorable action by other agencies (in this case the chief executive, administering bureaucracies, and the courts) which may simply not exist in reality. Some agencies may be predisposed against acting on a particular issue, or they may simply assign lower priority to an issue than other agencies do.

For example, the question of how best to maintain control over government information-gathering, spying, and foreign covert activities may be important to Congress and the Supreme Court, but the president may regard it as a minor issue, and the FBI and the CIA may be disinclined to submit to greater control no matter what anyone else says. The same problem of divergent perspectives sometimes occurs even within a single agency. Before the congressional budget committees came into existence in 1975, the separation of congressional decision making between substantive and appropriations committees sometimes left new programs, such as the 1965 rent supplements program, temporarily without funds as the appropriations committees fought a rear guard action against the congressional majority.

The fact of divergent official agendas can be both beneficial and detrimental to the resolution of social issues. It is beneficial in that it allows access to official agendas by a wider variety of social issue publics than would be the case if all governmental agencies were bound together by common perspectives. However, achieving access to one official agenda may be a hollow victory if accommodation with other government agencies proves impossible. Groups with access to different parts of the policy process may be able to veto each other's proposals, but veto power does not lead to the resolution of social issues when the diverging points of views are represented on competing agendas.

It is sometimes argued that certain kinds of political organizations, like political parties and interest group coalitions, operate midway between citizen groups and governmental institutions and serve to bridge the institutional gaps that would otherwise plague the resolution of social issues. This function, sometimes called interest aggregation, is undoubtedly important, but there is reason to believe that the agenda-unifying potential of parties and group coalitions is limited.[9] The bread and butter of political parties is not the ephemeral issue but the enduring social cleavage with its roots deep in geographic tradition or social and economic class. Similarly, interest group coalitions tend to reflect these same social divisions as they reassert themselves in the context of current social issues. These enduring issues—how much should income be redistributed? how extensive should public social services be? how much freedom should private enterprise be allowed? how hard should governments try to prevent class, ethnic, and racial prejudice?—form part but not the whole of the governmental agenda, and they are really never resolved completely. The issues most capable of resolution in a short time span are also those for which these stable partisan and group affiliations do not usually help very much. At most, parties and party platforms are access devices, and the group struggle surrounding party platforms is an agenda-setting process, not one for resolving issues. A number of issues are drafted into party platforms year after year; if this fact *alone* were at all important they would long since have been resolved.

For all political institutions, the contents of the official agenda are known farthest in advance for the most routine items. In every instance it is possible to push emergency questions onto the agenda, and indeed, to the top of the agenda, by extraordinary procedures. The routine business of government is probably least relevant for the resolution of social issues, however,

[9] Roger W. Cobb and Charles D. Elder, *Participation in American Politics: The Dynamics of Agenda Building,* Boston, Allyn and Bacon, Inc., 1972, p. 91.

while the scheduling of expedited decisions or pressing social issues is such that knowing they are on an official agenda tells us little about the likely outcome of the decision. Thus the timing of the next budgetary allocation for urban employment programs is well known, and the nature of the decision can be predicted; but the occurrence of the next urban riots, or the governmental response to them, can scarcely be guessed at.

The difficulty here is not with the notion of an agenda; that is valid enough. The problem comes with the concept of agenda-setting, because it implies a single mind deciding what will be on the agenda, establishing priorities and deadlines for action on agenda items. The process is more complicated in reality. Getting an issue on the public agenda or an official agenda is an achievement, but the credit must go to a large and ill-coordinated assortment of political actors. And rather than one coalition carrying through from setting the agenda to implementing decisions, those instrumental in getting items put on an agenda must share, delegate, or give over their interest in actual decisions to yet another diverse group of political actors.

Decisions, Responses, and Beyond

It is easy enough to follow an issue from a place on the official agenda to a resulting policy decision. Individual decisions cannot, however, be equated with issue resolutions. The terms of an isolated decision usually do not replicate the complexity of the original issue. The typical policy decision continues, terminates, or modifies an existing program, or it responds to a specific and limited aspect of a broader social issue. Decision processes and decision makers, at least human ones, have difficulty considering several options simultaneously, and cautious politicians are usually suspicious of moving more than one step at a time. Thus a program's funding level may be set separately from its operational details, and these in turn may be set separately from the program's basic principles. Administrative devices may, for example, be chosen separately from the delimitation of the program's beneficiaries.

Despite the many opportunities for amending a proposal before its final passage, the terms of a decision almost always come down to some kind of yes or no choice. The politician who honestly feels that "Yes, but . . ." is the best answer is almost certain to be dissatisfied. Thus the congressman who wanted an antiballistic missile system but not ABM, or who wanted welfare reform but not FAP, or who felt tax reform was needed but not the Ford rebate, or who wanted different school aid formulas, or different controls on abortion, or different procedures for school integration—these politicians faced a classic dilemma. They could oppose the alternatives offered in hope of getting something better, but then nothing might be done for lack of unified support. They could accept one of the offered alternatives, but then they would give up the chance to force something better by requiring proponents of change to modify their proposals and submit them again. Thus an isolated decision, because it can offer only a limited choice, will often be either an imperfect or a partial issue resolution.

The reaction of issue claimants to isolated policy decisions may vary greatly. If they feel they have been successful, claimants can sit back and congratulate themselves while waiting to see that the decision is carried through into actual policy. If they were not on the winning side, their next move depends on continuing support from the issue public in whose name they have been laboring.

The preferred strategy, if the supporting public will accept it, is to adopt a long time perspective. Of course the public may *not* accept it, for good reason. Realistically considered, major policy innovations often require many years from proposal to adoption and adjustment based on actual operating experience. Assumptions about the long run are notoriously unreliable in politics. For example, Cronin reports the prevalence of a somewhat naive "two term strategy" among White House staff members in the Johnson administration.[10] They planned to fill the law books with new programs in the first term and then devote the second

[10] Cronin, *The State of the Presidency,* p. 167.

term to solving administrative and implementation problems. In the event, what would have been Johnson's second term was managed by Richard Nixon and his appointees, with quite different results.

What, then, do issue entrepreneurs do in immediate reaction to failure? If resources allow, they may be tempted into a compensatory flurry of activity. By shifting their strategic target to different access points or different levels of government, petitioning groups can continue their efforts with scarcely a break in momentum. More commonly, however, groups adjust their strategies to the yearly cycles of governmental decision making. The complete unfolding of next year's strategy must wait for an assessment of possible changes in the political environment— changed public concerns, party shifts, changes in administrative personnel, and so on. At most, some contingency planning can be done in advance.

There is really no final step in the issue translation process, because the results of policy decisions, whether they resolve social issues or not, return to society and disappear in the maze of forces from which may eventually emerge further issue claims. It is impossible to do more than set arbitrary bounds on the long-term effects of a particular policy decision since all decisions change group strategies somewhat, alter objective social conditions (perhaps for the better), and modify the interests of various groups in ways that would be very difficult to trace.

Nevertheless, it is possible to identify two situations in which we can be sure that some further political activity *will* take place. In the first instance, an issue resolution cannot be effective unless and until it is actually implemented. A great deal of political virtuosity is squandered on legislative coalition building; no such virtue is recognized for bureaucratic application of policy decisions although this is every bit as necessary a step. Of course, implementation is not a simple yes or no matter. Some effort will usually be put into the task of carrying out legislative intentions, but there is no guarantee that all parties involved will be satisfied with the results of this effort. "Implementation failure" thus has a general similarity to an issue that seems to have been ignored, as far as its political consequences are concerned, and the examples cited in Chapter 6 may serve as a guide to the political dynamics of such cases.

In the second instance, a resolution will probably not be recognized as such, even if it subsequently proves highly effective in practice, if one or more issue publics is convinced that it was not the right action to take. The political effects of such "wrong resolutions" may be likened to those of issues that are in fact ignored, because it makes little difference to an unsatisfied group whether its request was carefully considered and rejected or it was never really considered. The examples cited in Chapter 7 illustrate how some groups have responded under similar circumstances.

To summarize the general picture of the translation process, we can consider, finally, some evidence of the time dimension and patterns of actor involvement in issue politics. The next two chapters then expand on the varieties of governmental response—and nonresponse—that underlie these dynamics of the issue translation process.

The Dimensions of Issue Translation

The overall issue translation process, if we follow it backward to the emergence of an issue and forward to its resolution, encompasses a number of distinguishable steps (Figure 1). These may be squeezed into a short time span or stretched over a long period, depending on the level of public controversy and the rate of success in reaching compromises at each point along the line. The density of activity may likewise vary greatly, depending both on "internal" events (such as compromises) and external events (such as the timing of elections).

Table 3 shows the range of variation among four recent major issues.[11] Of the four, abortion is not yet resolved and appears to be continuing with a high level of public and governmental activity (Table 4). Amnesty, a largely resolved issue, shows a clear shift from public to governmental actions within a short time

---

[11] I wish to acknowledge the assistance of Rob Stiglicz in the collection of the raw data for these issues.

Figure 1: The Issue Translation Process in Ideal Form

1. A social problem	4. becomes a social issue	5. achieves a place on the public agenda	7. is placed on an official agenda	8. and a policy decision of some kind is made	9. groups may pursue a related issues strategy
2. perceived by groups	3. is joined by groups with differing opinions	(issue entre-preneurs are active here)		6. by the actions of issue entre-preneurs	or wait to try the same strategy in the next round
			(more groups may join here)		

Table 3
Patterns of Issue Politics Over Time

Number of Events Per Year	Issue Area Pornography	Amnesty	Abortion	Gun Control
Year 1	1	14	1	1
2	5	7	0	2
3	18	23	2	4
4	12	13	0	26
5	1		13	4
6	8		7	4
7	5		12	7
8	5		31	16
9			12	7
10			28	2
11			9	8
12			20	
13			18	

Source: Facts on File.
Pornography, year 1 = 1968.
Amnesty, year 1 = 1972.
Abortion, year 1 = 1963.
Gun Control, year 1 = 1965.

span. Pornography shows a similar shift, but at a slower rate. Public actions preceded governmental in both abortion and gun control, showing movement from a public to a governmental agenda, but nongovernmental action continued at a high rate, especially for abortion.

The varieties of governmental involvement in these four issue areas (Table 5) reveal additional dimensions of the translation process. To begin with, amnesty presents a simple instance of a completely nationalized, completely "legislated" issue—no involvement by state or local governments or the courts (see "decisions that appear to be only symbolic," Chapter 6). Court involvement is sporadic but much more extensive in the pornography question, while state and local government activity is still minor.

Table 4
Actor Involvement in Public Issues Over Time

Number of Events Per Year	Issue Area Pornography		Amnesty		Abortion		Gun Control	
	Gov	Nongov	Gov	Nongov	Gov	Nongov	Gov	Nongov
Year 1	1	0	6	8	0	1	0	1
2	4	1	3	4	0	0	1	1
3	13	5	15	8	0	2	3	1
4	10	2	10	3	0	0	13	13
5	1	0			7	6	1	3
6	7	1			2	5	4	0
7	5	0			8	4	6	1
8	5	0			20	11	10	6
9					2	10	3	4
10					15	13	1	1
11					6	3	7	1
12					9	11		
13					11	7		

Source: Facts on File.
  Pornography, year 1 = 1968.
  Amnesty, year 1 = 1972.
  Abortion, year 1 = 1963.
  Gun Control, year 1 = 1965.

Separating the several types of government action, as Table 5 does, helps to reveal the success or failure of attempted resolutions. For instance, in pornography there is a great peak of legislative and executive action in 1970, coinciding with the report of the Commission on Obscenity and Pornography (see "the old ways are good enough," Chapter 3), but the courts still had to work out case-by-case decisions.

Abortion, in the evidence of Table 5, is an essentially local issue into which first the courts and then the national legislative and executive branches have been increasingly drawn (see: "decisions not to intervene," Chapter 6). Continuing activity at all levels shows that the issue has not yet been resolved, however.

Table 5
Government Involvement in Public Issues Over Time

Issue Area and Type of Actor	Number of Events Per Year Year												
	1	2	3	4	5	6	7	8	9	10	11	12	13
Pornography													
leg/exec	1	1	8	2	0	1	0	0					
courts	0	2	5	8	0	6	3	4					
state/local	0	1	0	0	1	0	2	1					
Amnesty													
(all governmental involvement was legislative or executive)													
Abortion													
leg/exec	0	0	0	0	0	0	0	0	1	2	2	3	4
courts	0	0	0	0	0	0	0	3	1	1	4	2	4
state/local	0	0	0	0	7	2	8	17	0	12	0	4	3
Gun Control													
leg/exec	0	1	2	11	0	1	0	7	2	1	5		
courts	0	0	0	1	0	0	4	1	0	0	1		
state/local	0	0	1	1	1	3	2	2	1	0	1		

Source: Facts on File.
  Pornography, year 1 = 1968.
  Amnesty, year 1 = 1972.
  Abortion, year 1 = 1963.
  Gun Control, year 1 = 1965.

Finally, gun control shows a highly variable pattern of government activity. Court involvement is generally low, and legislative activity at the national level is very sporadic. The two peaks, in 1968 and 1972, coincide with assassinations and other gun-related events arousing public concern (see "politics as usual," Chapter 7), but the ultimate response failure in both instances is revealed by continuing activity, both governmental and non-governmental (Table 4).

At best, the data in Tables 3,4, and 5 can only show the pattern of activity surrounding an issue. Variety is the keynote for the issue areas discussed: the intensity of activity, its location, and its duration all vary greatly in ways that can be understood most readily by referring to the issues themselves. The further questions of how response can be achieved, and what kinds of response can reasonably be expected, are discussed in the remainder of this book.

6

Why Many Issues Seem to Be Ignored

The next two chapters illustrate a variety of outcomes for social issues. Beyond simply showing the diversity of issue responses, they seek to distinguish broadly between real-but-unsatisfying responses and failures-to-respond. In the first instance, the issue translation process has produced a decision; in the second, the process has been cut short. In neither instance has the issue been truly resolved; consequently it cannot be argued with complete confidence that the action so far observed is the final governmental word on the subject. When there has been some response, even if unsatisfactory, the groups and issue publics mobilized for participation in the translation process will probably carry through. When there has been no response, issue publics must start again at the beginning if they want to see anything concrete for their efforts.

The missing category in these chapters is the successfully resolved issue. The reason for concentrating on cases of failure is simply that lessons can be learned more readily by isolating shortcomings than by showing how successfully resolved issues passed through the steps of the issue translation process. The list of 47 issues from Chapter 1 will give some idea how frequently issues *are* resolved, and will suggest the relative importance of the various kinds of response failure. The results, shown in Table 6, reflect generous identification of the various kinds of

Table 6
Disposition of a Sample of Issues

Disposition	Issues of Governmental Role		Inherently Political Issues	
Successfully resolved	(7)	26%	(10)	50%
Seemingly ignored		37%		35%
no intervention	(3)		(1)	
symbolic response	(2)		(2)	
unexpected response	(1)		(0)	
delayed response	(2)		(3)	
response at another level	(2)		(1)	
Actually ignored		37%		15%
vague demands	(3)		(1)	
issues not for gov't	(1)		(0)	
politics as usual	(6)		(2)	
	(27)	100%	(20)	100%

Source: See text.

unsatisfactory response, so some of the issues listed there may have subsequently moved into the "successfully resolved" category.

In Table 6 the governmental role issues clearly differ from those in which government involvement is inevitable. Political issues are noticeably more likely to be resolved, and less likely to be ignored, than basically social issues. In part this distinction reflects the definition of official agendas. Issues in which governmental involvement is inevitable often come before the public as a consequence of reaction to prior governmental action, thus they become issues when they can no longer be ignored. Resolution is also easier to identify in many instances of inherently political issues because the nature of governmental involvement means that definite governmental decisions must occur. Nominations, impeachments, pardons, specific acts of war all result in decisions that are both authoritative and self-enforcing, and therefore likely to bring controversy to an end more surely than decisions on regulatory and social policy issues.

Overall, the results of this tabulation are not greatly encouraging. Roughly equal proportions of issues are ignored, responded to with less than complete success, and successfully disposed of. The specific figures are only as good as the list of 47 issues is representative, and the judgment of outcomes is accurate, but the general distribution of outcomes must be some indication of governmental effectiveness at translating issues into public policy in a manner acceptable to the American public. Of course, the results are limited by the time span chosen, and some of the most recently occurring issues may be brought to a successful conclusion in the near future. But for every such issue there is probably at least one other previously resolved issue that may come unstuck as subsequent events unfold. At any moment, then, perhaps one issue out of three has a good chance of successful resolution, another one of every three is working its way toward some kind of partial conclusion, and the remaining one of three is being ignored.

Decisions Not to Intervene

The abortion issue ("should therapeutic abortions be allowed, and if so, under what conditions?") illustrates the difficulties in resolving a social issue when the groups on one side of an issue are determined to have their own way, and when the most authoritative government policy makers steadfastly refuse to consider the issue. There has been a great deal of action on abortion at the state and federal levels over the years, but never has a definitive decision been made.

Abortion control legislation at the state level dates back to 1821. At one time or another, all but four of the states have enacted laws generally prohibiting abortions unless the life of the mother is endangered. The apparent rationale for this prohibition was the considerable danger attending any surgical procedure in the nineteenth century, with the inappropriateness of controlling population growth or encouraging sexual promiscuity as secondary reasons. Advances in medical technique complicated the question by greatly reducing the danger in abortions, reducing the health risk of pregnancy, and pushing back the stage of development at which a human fetus might live if prematurely taken from the mother.

In the late 1960s, a number of states began liberalizing their abortion laws to allow abortions under a wider range of conditions. Proponents of reform brought legal action or proposed legislative changes in some 20 states, and several state courts struck down state laws as invading the right to privacy (based on the U.S. Supreme Court's decision in *Griswold v. Connecticut* in 1965 that prohibition of the use of contraceptives by married couples invaded their privacy) or as being unconstitutionally vague (in response to changing medical definitions of the onset of life). Reform proposals were introduced in Congress in 1969 and 1970.

State-by-state actions continued erratically while several test cases made their way through the federal courts. *Doe v. Bolton* and *Roe v. Wade* were argued before the U.S. Supreme Court in 1971 and again in 1972. In both cases, lower federal courts had ruled state antiabortion laws unconstitutional. The Supreme Court ruled on these cases in January 1973 to the effect that states could not interfere with decisions to abort made by a woman and her doctor in the first trimester of pregnancy, that they had a limited range of control in the second trimester, and that abortions could be prohibited constitutionally only during the last trimester of pregnancy.

The Doe and Roe decisions left many unanswered questions, and a number of states kept their laws, or enacted new ones, stating that doctors and hospitals could not be forced to perform abortions against their moral beliefs. Several bills were introduced in Congress to amend the Constitution to extend constitutional rights to unborn children, or to affirm state prerogatives to prohibit abortions despite any other interpretation of the Constitution, but congressional committees sat on these proposals during 1973. Congress did enact one provision stating that medical institutions and personnel receiving federal health money (except Medicare) could not be forced against religious or moral beliefs to perform abortions.

The shift to Congress following the Supreme Court ruling in 1973 gave substantial impetus to national lobbying coalitions, many of which had previously been just loose associations of state and local groups. Those in favor of abortion reform included Planned Parenthood, the National Abortion Rights Action League, the Religious Coalition for Abortion Rights, and two more broadly based groups: the American Civil Liberties Union and the National Organization for Women. On the other side of the question were the Ad Hoc Committee in Defense of Life, the National Conference of Catholic Bishops, the National Committee for a Human Life Amendment, and the National Right to Life Committee.

Congressional hearings were held in 1974 and 1975, but no further action was taken on proposed antiabortion amendments to the Constitution. Efforts to prohibit use of Medicaid funds for abortions for welfare recipients were finally successful in 1976,[1] after having been defeated in 1974 and 1975, when Congress overrode President Ford's veto of a Labor-HEW appropriations bill to which the amendment had been added. Meanwhile, state legislatures continued to challenge the Supreme Court ruling by redrafting statutes to construe the ruling as narrowly as possible, or in some cases to challenge it directly. Perhaps taking their cue from this upsurge of state activity, Congressmen drifted toward a "states rights" amendment on abortion that would give the ultimate decision back to the states, at the same time relieving the Congress of the need to take a definite position on the underlying moral questions.

Why is it that the abortion issue has not been resolved, despite the great expenditure of effort at both state and federal levels? The answer obviously is that Congress has refused to act definitively on the abortion question, and until it does so the disgruntled losers can always hope that Congress will eventually be forced to act if the issue can be kept alive by court challenges and lobbying pressures. Once the antiabortion groups hit upon the constitutional amendment idea, they committed their efforts to a strategy that would force congressional action if it could be sustained. At the same time, however, abortion opponents hope that significant changes in court rulings will occur if the issue drags on long enough. New judges on the court, or court stale-

---

[1] Implementation of the fund cutoff was delayed until 1977 by a court injunction.

mate produced by efforts to resolve the unanswered questions of the Roe and Doe decision, may produce conditions favorable to the reintroduction of strict abortion controls.

Decisions That Appear to Be Only Symbolic

There is probably no objective way to determine whether a concrete policy response is real or symbolic. Underfunded programs and other forms of token response—throwing a crust of bread when a loaf is needed—are often criticized for being only symbolic; that is, for being consciously designed to provide only the appearance of responsiveness. Ambiguity enters because the ultimate test is not the policy makers' intentions but the impact of the policy, and responses intended to be only symbolic may produce real results if the target groups believe the responses to be real and react accordingly.

To be completely fair to politicians, perhaps we should say that every policy has both a verbal and an effective component. The verbal component states the policy's purpose and expresses the policy makers' intention to respond, while the effective component is that part—whether regulatory rules, grants in aid, or whatever—that has direct impact on the policy's target groups. For perfectly understandable political reasons, politicians sometimes put forward the verbal policy and then find themselves unable to deliver the effect. The policy is only symbolic in effect even though there were honest intentions to follow through and produce results. It is just those few cases where politicians have cynically pledged their verbal intentions with no real commitment to act that can be criticized for being "only symbolic."

The Ford administration's amnesty program for Vietnam era draft resisters and evaders is an example of a policy response with substantial symbolic intentions. First proposed 10 days after Ford took office in 1974, and implemented by proclamation a month later, the plan initially aroused opposition by unfavorable association with the Nixon pardon announced a week earlier. Expecting draft resisters and evaders to earn their reentry into American society by alternate service up to two years in duration, while the former president escaped any further investigation or punishment, was criticized as unfair. Since the sincerity (and effectiveness) of the Nixon pardon could not be doubted, doubt was instead thrown on the sincerity of the amnesty program.

The Ford program, always described officially as "clemency" rather than "amnesty," had some explicitly symbolic intentions. The proclamation stated its major purpose to be "the reconciliation of all our people and the restoration of the essential unity of Americans," not by condoning desertion or draft evasion, but by "an act of mercy to bind the nation's wounds and to heal the scars of divisiveness." In short, its effect was to be felt among all Americans, including a great many who never served in the military during Vietnam and never had any member of their family in service.

Further evidence that the clemency plan was intended largely for symbolic effect was its timing. Coming so soon after Ford took office, it emphasized the contrast with Nixon's position, which had always been that evaders and deserters should suffer the full and appropriate legal penalties.[2] The appointment of former Senator Charles Goodell to chair the Presidential Clemency Board, however, worried opponents of amnesty. Goodell's strong antiwar position while in the Senate suggested to them that the clemency board would be overly lenient, and even that the workability of any future military draft would be jeopardized if draft evaders from the Vietnam era got home free. The original deadline of January 31, 1975—giving exiles somewhat more than four months to come home and surrender—was an ambiguous indicator of the plan's true intentions. The time period was short enough that exiles would have to act, in many cases, without any clear picture of how the clemency board was interpreting its responsibilities, but it was consistent with President Ford's announced hope that the clemency program and the Nixon pardon would quickly put the war and Watergate behind us.

In the event, the clemency program was less than a complete success. The complexity of its procedures and the initially slow

[2] Robert Weissberg, *Public Opinion and Popular Government,* Englewood Cliffs, N.J., Prentice-Hall, Inc., 1976, pp. 235–7.

response led to a two month extension of the deadline for application for clemency. Even with the extension, between 75% and 80% of the armed services members eligible for clemency failed to apply. Most of these were service personnel who had received undesirable discharges for being AWOL. They were eligible to apply to change their status to that of "clemency discharge," but they saw little evidence that this change would substantially affect their employability, and it would not make them eligible to receive veterans benefits. In addition, some substantial groups of people, both civilian and military, who had suffered for their beliefs about the war were not included in the clemency program. About 5000 deserters who had already renounced their citizenship were not included, nor were servicemen who received less than honorable discharges for misconduct other than desertion, nor were any of the civilians who ran afoul of the law while protesting the war. An effort to bury all traces of the war might have dealt with these groups, and several were proposed in Congress in 1975, but none got beyond the committee stage.

Table 7 summarizes the disposition of the cases processed by the clemency board. The figures belie any notion that the board was instructed to grant blanket amnesty, but they also indicate

Table 7

Disposition of Applications for Clemency, 1974–1975

Pardons requiring more than 12 months alternate service	3	Completed obligation	115
		Presently serving	1850
		Waiting to serve	1160
Pardons requiring up to 12 months service	7600	Broke agreement to serve	2407
Pardons requiring no service	6400	Have not agreed to serve	2071
Pardons denied	900		
Ineligible	5950		
Open cases (transferred to Justice Department)	600		
Total applications processed	21,500		

Data as of September 15, 1975, when funding authority for the Clemency Board expired.

that many applicants chose to reject the conditional pardons offered to them in return for alternate service. In the end, the program must have failed to persuade them that the requirement of alternate service was fair, or that the rewards were worth the effort. Perhaps many of them, with no hope of receiving the veterans benefits that their comrades in arms enjoyed, discounted the significance of pardon from a government whose moral position they disagreed with.

The amnesty program failed, finally, in its symbolic mission to reconcile the nation because it failed in its more concrete efforts to reenlist the loyalty of draft evaders and deserters and persuade them to earn a position in American society again. Of course the war was forgotten eventually by all except servicemen who suffered personal loss, or their families, but only because it was displaced by more pressing domestic issues and personal concerns. The amnesty program attempted to respond to a real problem, but in the end it could not overcome the strong moral positions taken on both sides of the issue.

The symbolic element in politics is more pervasive than may often be realized. Under some circumstances, as Murray Edelman has pointed out, social groups may even seek out symbolic reassurance.[3] A group will do so, according to Edelman, when it feels threatened but lacks the political power necessary to force a real response. Harold Lasswell provides the psychological motive for this phenomenon by emphasizing the distinction between individual wants and individual needs.[4] When individuals do not understand their real needs, they will seek to divert their wants by the magical use of sacred political symbols.

As an example of this kind of symbolic response, Edelman quotes Thurman Arnold's discussion of the antitrust laws and Theodore Roosevelt's trust-busting crusades.[5] Ripley and Franklin discuss a more recent example, that of the Federal

[3] Murray Edelman, *The Symbolic Uses of Politics,* Urbana, University of Illinois Press, 1964, pp. 22–43.

[4] Harold D. Lasswell, *Psychopathology and Politics,* New York, The Viking Press, 1960, p. 194.

[5] Thurman W. Arnold, *The Folklore of Capitalism,* New Haven, Yale University Press, 1959, Chapter IX.

Trade Commission and the health lobby campaign against the tobacco industry.[6] They argue that the cancer warning printed on cigarette packages is only a symbolic response to the health problems associated with tobacco. Consumerism often has strongly symbolic overtones because consumers pose a potential electoral threat but they lack the organizational power necessary to make legitimate gains and to support the government bureaucracies working on their behalf.[7]

The writers on symbolism in public policy all agree that symbolic responses are effective in producing quiescence among target groups. Symbolic reassurance *is* satisfying, especially if there is no realistic prospect of anything concrete.

The argument can be carried one important step further. Official symbolic reassurances persuade the powerless groups being reassured that policy is successful, but they also conceal the lack of real achievement from other, more powerful groups that might otherwise step in. Thus the symbolic elements in antitrust and social welfare policies, for example, have probably hampered union and liberal group involvement in these issues, or at least diverted their attention to reform targets that do not challenge the fundamental assumptions in these policy areas.

Disappointing Decisions; Confounding Results

Politics can be a very discouraging business for anyone—citizen or politician—who expects to get everything asked for and nothing else. Interest groups and issue publics hoping to achieve all their goals in a single court term or legislative session will certainly get less than this; in some cases they may get a hearing and nothing else, or the promise of a test case, in others they may get part of what they ask, or an ambiguous ruling that must be pursued further through the courts in subsequent terms.

Because incrementalism is a favorite American political strategy, "incremental despair" may be the most common form

[6] Randall B. Ripley and Grace A. Franklin, *Congress, The Bureaucracy, and Public Policy*, Homewood, Ill., The Dorsey Press, 1976, pp. 82–4.

[7] Mark V. Nadel, "Unorganized Interests and the Politics of Consumer Protection," pp. 148–68 in Michael P. Smith and associates, *Politics in America: Studies in Policy Analysis*, New York, Random House, 1974.

of disappointment, and therefore of feelings that issues have not been responded to adequately. But these feelings are often misleading. At worst, a thorough-going incrementalism creates a series of small disappointments, while at the same time holding out the promise that all claimants will see policy move gradually closer to their own position if they persevere. Starting with nothing, the group committed to the legislative battle may eventually achieve a great deal if it pursues an issue that can be segmented in a manner appropriate for incremental response.

Politicians are not usually disheartened if change is only incremental. They find, if the issue is appropriate, that their political rewards will parallel the expansion of an incremental bargain. If they somehow manage to satisfy one interest group completely, it would only be necessary to find another to which to demonstrate their coalition-making abilities.

Unfortunately it is often not enough to gain a favorable decision. Results may confound as well. The mere fact of having achieved a policy response is no guarantee that the expected consequences will follow. Some issues remain on the public agenda for many years, despite repeated attempts to resolve them, while the level of concern and the urgency of the issue fluctuate and even the precise statement of the issue changes with time. There are at least three reasons why issues may persist in this way, and why there may be dissatisfaction with attempted issue resolutions no matter how honest they are.

1. The resolution of one issue may alter the balance of political forces and make possible the raising and resolving of a related issue. For instance, an interest group or a coalition of groups formed for one issue may also prove necessary for further issues, and once the group has achieved an initial success it will be inclined to look around for new areas in which to make its impact felt.

2. The resolution of one issue may simply reveal a further barrier to achieving the goals sought by issue publics. The root of a problem of this kind may be the phenomenon of multiple causation—when the easiest or the most obvious issue is resolved, further issues appear in its place and new causes of the original problem emerge as the target for a revival of

controversy. The appearance of one closed door behind another may eventually weary the groups seeking change, although they and their allies of the moment may be encouraged from time to time by their periodic successes.

3. The resolution of one issue may generate further issues because the specific means chosen to resolve the first issue had unexpected side effects which precipitated another controversy. This Pandora's box phenomenon may occur when governments move into uncharted waters in response to political pressures to resolve a standing issue. All participants are acting in good faith, and they all believe (or at least hope) that they are acting to resolve a major conflict.

The history of the Bail Reform Act of 1966 provides a good illustration of a Pandora's box problem that did eventually reach a resolution. The 1966 act was a liberal measure affecting federal courts. It provided for pretrial release of criminal suspects without money bail unless there was reason to think they would not return for trial. The law's basic purpose was to reduce the large monetary and space burden imposed by pretrial incarceration. By eliminating money bail in most cases, it also curtailed the discriminatory effects of the bail system, where professional criminals and middle class suspects could usually go free pending trial but poor suspects could not afford to bail themselves out.

The effects of the act were particularly noticeable in Washington, D.C., the only federal jurisdiction handling a large number of violent crimes. There, large numbers of suspects awaiting trial were released without bail, and they promptly went about their business committing more crimes while awaiting trial for their first offenses. Initial presidential reaction to these problems, in 1969, provided greater freedom for judges in using pretrial detention and, for the District of Columbia, involved a court reorganization plan and an expansion of the police force.

In the District of Columbia the bail issue was muddled with the general problems of a high crime rate, and bail reform became part of an omnibus D.C. crime bill that increased sentences for many felonies, stiffened juvenile justice procedures, and provided for wiretapping and no knock entry in addition to court reform and a 60 day pretrial detention period for persons suspected of violent crimes. To some extent, these provisions work against each other, for greater police powers should increase the trial backlog and put extra pressure on the detention period. At the same time, there is reason to believe that the pretrial offender problem had been used as an excuse to support the detention plan. A Justice Department study released during the lengthy hearings on the D.C. omnibus crime bill showed that rearrests during the pretrial period occurred for only 11.7% of all offenders on bail.

In any event, the 1966 bail reform plan was ultimately beneficial even though its immediate impact on the crime rate was detrimental. Evaluation of the effects of bail reform highlighted another weak spot in the system, and judges were able to make use of the reform momentum to secure a much-needed court reorganization. Opponents of preventive detention insisted successfully on the inclusion of expedited trial procedures for offenders under the 60 day detention provisions, although they were forced to accept no knock entry provisions.[8]

A second, even shorter example may illustrate the doors-behind-doors problem. The federal government's efforts in school desegregation and general aid to elementary and secondary schools share the goal of equalizing educational opportunity, especially for racial and ethnic minority groups living in core cities. Over the years, however, the church-state question has posed a legal and political barrier to full achievement of this goal. In particular, Title I of the Elementary and Secondary Education Act of 1965, the basic aid program for urban and rural disadvantaged children, adopted a tortuous definition of its target population in order to avoid defeat on the church-state question. School districts could not be aided directly, for this would mean leaving out religious schools and risking defeat of ESEA at the hands of legislators who had large numbers of constituents sending their children to parochial schools. Aid could not be given directly to segregated schools, for this would

[8] Congress repealed these provisions in 1974.

violate Title VI of the 1964 Civil Rights Act. So ESEA identified
its target group as disadvantaged children rather than low income school districts, and directed aid money to areas within
large city school systems where low income families were concentrated.

The liabilities of the ESEA formula become clear when school
districts attempt to move children from one school building to
adjacent ones in order to improve racial balance in the schools,
or to offer all students a wider choice of educational methods
and resources than could be provided by any one school building. Reassignment of students disperses the concentration of
poor aid recipients on which Title I is targeted and risks a possible loss of eligibility for aid, yet the purpose of reassignment is to
make more efficient use of the aid money. ESEA Title I would
probably be more effective if local districts were allowed to apply
it flexibly in pursuit of quality integrated education, and in fact
failure to comply exactly with ESEA guidelines has been a widespread local district response.[9]

A final example, drawn from federal housing legislation,
shows further problems in the linkage between intentions and
outcomes. Two broad patterns in public housing policies have
been apparent over the years. First, so-called public housing
programs have proliferated and diffused until they can scarcely
be distinguished from other federal housing efforts. Both target
groups and strategies have expanded in an attempt to correct
new problems as they arise. Second, nearly every program has
encountered the same kinds of problems, all resulting from economic or political restrictions on federal policy.

The original public housing program, created by the Housing
Acts of 1937 and 1949, operates through local housing authorities. With the assistance of federal loans and annual subsidy
payments, the housing authorities build and manage public
housing for low-income families. Legislation in 1959 added a

---

[9] The early history of ESEA is reviewed by Eugene Eidenberg and Roy D. Morey,
An Act of Congress, New York, W. W. Norton, 1969, and Stephen K. Bailey and
Edith K. Mosher, *ESEA: The Office of Education Administers a Law,* Syracuse,
Syracuse University Press, 1968. See also Norman C. Thomas, *Education in
National Politics,* New York, David McKay Company, Inc., 1975.

program of direct low interest loans to nursing homes and private nonprofit corporations for construction of rental housing for the elderly. Consumer cooperatives and public agencies were made eligible for this program in 1961. The Housing Act of 1964 added a grant program to pay up to two-thirds of the cost of developing low rent housing for domestic farm workers.

Dissatisfaction with the quality of public housing and frustration with the slow rate of construction of low rent housing led to the controversial rent supplements program in 1965. In effect, this program increased the shelter purchasing power of low-income families, thereby stimulating the supply of low rent housing units. Rent supplements were first funded in 1966, which was also the first year of a new program of grants and loans to the state of Alaska for the construction of housing for natives and other needy persons. Most recently, the Housing and Urban Development Act of 1968 created two new programs to subsidize mortgage interest rates to allow low-income families to buy homes, and to subsidize mortgage interest costs for nonprofit corporations constructing low rent housing. These last two programs were the only ones intended to replace previous efforts: when fully funded they were expected to replace the 1959 direct low interest loan program.

This chronology is just the barest outline of those programs that merit inclusion as low income public housing. Parallel to these were a number of moderate-income housing programs and the familiar FHA and VA mortgage guarantees open to all income levels. Each of these programs, as it was carried forward from one year to the next, required frequent adjustment to avoid conflicts with other public housing programs, and each underwent adjustment of eligibility rules, benefit levels, administrative changes, and altered relationships to urban renewal and Model Cities efforts running simultaneously in many cities under the stimulative effect of federal funds. Unfortunately, this long series of incremental changes rarely seemed to produce a better public housing effort. Instead, the programs became less effective as they grew in complexity. Toward the end of the 1960s, Congress almost gave up its efforts to understand and manage the housing program, deferring more and more to the housing bureaucracy.

Sooner or later, all the separate public housing efforts came to grief because they attempted to work through lending banks, private developers, and other private institutions already active in the housing field. The government, especially the Federal Housing Administration, was outmaneuvered legally and illegally and left holding the pieces. The section 235 and 236 programs created in 1968 were the most notorious in this regard, leaving the FHA as landlord of a quarter of a million decaying housing units after little more than four years of operation. The process was often ridiculously simple. A speculator would buy a rundown house, make a few superficial repairs, persuade FHA to approve a mortgage loan on it, and sell it at an inflated price. When the house began to fall apart and the new owner could not keep up mortgage payments and repair costs, the mortgage loan was defaulted and the FHA took over.

Faced with this disaster, President Nixon in 1973 declared a moratorium on further federal commitments to public housing until more workable schemes could be devised. Yet the public housing programs did not fail for lack of trying. If there is a single reason (aside from human frailty) for public housing difficulties, it is that the programs labored under an impossible but seemingly rational condition: they must operate through existing private financial institutions, or (where they were wholly governmental), they must not compete with and undercut the private housing market. Under these circumstances it is not surprising that the outcome confounded all expectations and could not in the end be rectified no matter how much tinkering was done.

Leonard Freedman, in his study of public housing politics, points out that the restrictive conditions under which public housing has suffered have been imposed by its political enemies.[10] In fact, the public housing coalition fell apart soon after the landmark 1949 act was passed, and the program's poor clientele lacked the political power necessary to insure that the act's goals were achieved. In this connection the change of emphasis from housing for the poor to relocation housing for

---

[10] Leonard Freedman, *Public Housing: The Politics of Poverty,* New York, Holt, Rinehart and Winston, 1969.

urban renewal projects, sponsored by the Eisenhower administration, indicated that the program had been captured by a local business-dominated coalition. This new requirement, plus conservative congressional appropriations committees, kept public housing construction at scarcely more than token level for many years. The programmatic innovations acceptable to the opponents of public housing were, by comparison with the original 1949 goals, relatively minor.

Delayed Responses

For many issues, especially those related to enduring social problems, there seems to be something like a natural, mandatory gestation period for issue responses. The inevitable impatience of claimant publics will lead them to claim nonresponse during this lengthy period even if their idea's time eventually does come. It is easy enough to sympathize with these groups because justice delayed *is* injustice, even if it is eventually set right, but there may be acceptable reasons for the delay that also warrant sympathy.

Why is it that issue responses are often so long in coming? The reasons are varied, of course, but usually the answer is that our expectations are unrealistically optimistic and not that the issue translation process is too slow. For instance, an effective response to the oil embargo required a long-range stockpiling program and a series of agreements with foreign powers over appropriate future responses to embargoes. Until these had been achieved, the critics claimed that no progress had been made on an energy policy. The control of corporate bribery by the foreign branches of American firms also required international negotiation and cooperation. To take a final example, achieving control over the American intelligence services may require extensive interference in their normal decision processes and lengthy, complicated negotiations among the different agencies involved—the FBI, CIA, National Security Agency, the Department of State and the diplomatic corps, and perhaps others.

A second reason for delay is the political barrier to a speedy decision created when group conflict brings in additional peripheral groups that must then be part of the final settlement. Political disagreements may also be overlaid with genuine reluctance to undertake untried approaches.

Both excuses were present at one time or another during the more than 20 years elapsing between the initial proposal of a federal fair employment commission and the final approval of enforcement powers for the commission. There were two distinct "gestation periods" in federal fair employment practices: the first, extending from 1944 to 1964, concerned the creation of a regular and permanent fair employment practices commission; the second, running from 1965 to 1972, concerned the provision of some kind of enforcement power for the federal fair employment agency created in 1964.

The seed for a federal fair employment policy was actually planted several years before any serious discussion of the question began, when President Roosevelt issued an executive order in 1941 requiring nondiscrimination in government employment and government contracts. The order declared that the government's implicit policy had already been nondiscrimination, so technically all the order did was to provide a specific operational form for the policy. In reality, the explicit policy statement was dictated in part by wartime conditions. The logic of civil rights group positions was that nondiscrimination in the military ought to be paralleled by equal job opportunity for the civilian members of minority groups who were contributing to the war effort during World War II.

The original fair employment program was extended twice in wartime circumstances before it was regularized by executive action in 1945. Between 1945 and 1964, the government employment and contracts antidiscriminatory policy was modified six times by executive order to add new client groups or to improve the coordinating and enforcing mechanisms within the executive branch.

Meanwhile, in 1944 and 1945 legislation was introduced and reported favorably from congressional committees to make the temporary wartime FEPC into a permanent civilian program with enforcement powers. When the wartime agency's authorization ran out and was not renewed by Congress, attention shifted to efforts to create an FEPC again. A total of eight proposals of this kind were sent to the floor of Congress before 1964. In addition, 26 states and several times that many cities adopted their own statutes forbidding employment discrimination. Throughout this period the main basis of opposition to FEPC proposals was that an FEPC would interfere extensively with legitimate business hiring decisions, or it would complicate the work of the state and local government agencies then being formed. This argument (whether honestly made or not) held sway over the critical committees and supported filibusters when necessary. On those grounds even a token FEPC was held off until 1964.

The breakthrough, when it did come, was simply part of a much larger coordinated set of policy requests covering nearly all aspects of civil rights. The motive force behind FEPC passage, and the coalition that supported it, was therefore something larger than the old opposition coalition. The legislation creating the Equal Employment Opportunity Commission was presented as Title VII of the 1964 Civil Rights Act. Its positive contributions to racial equality were emphasized, rather than the antidiscrimination approach of the earlier proposals. The omnibus strategy enlisted organized labor and a number of civil rights groups whose concern for equal employment prospects was only tangential, but the support of these groups for other parts of the bill—voting rights, for example—gave added political weight to the EEOC title.

The second gestation period ran from 1965 to 1972. In every one of these years, bills were introduced to allow enforcement powers to the EEOC, and committees reported favorably on such proposals four times before one was finally accepted in 1972. Enforcement powers had been deleted from the 1964 act in floor debate. Their addition was held up for several years by disagreement over the specific nature of enforcement powers, and also disagreement about the desirability of moving the Office of Federal Contract Compliance from the Department of Labor to the EEOC.

The enforcement powers question—whether to give EEOC

quasi-judicial cease and desist powers, or have it rely on court enforcement—was a classic regulatory enforcement dilemma. Congress split on the question, and the Senate Labor and Public Welfare Committee reported bills embodying both features in late 1971. President Nixon favored a court enforcement procedure, while 32 of the 37 state agencies with enforcement powers used a cease and desist procedure. Organized labor spokesmen did not take a strong position on the enforcement method, but they pushed hard for transfer of the Office of Federal Contract Compliance to EEOC. Their motive for the move, ostensibly justified by greater efficiency obtained through central direction of all civil rights enforcement in the employment area, apparently was to force a slowdown in the Philadelphia Plan for minority recruitment into the building trades. Unions resisted quota systems like the Philadelphia plan, and they seemed to feel that removing enforcement from the Department of Labor would slow the rate of quota-based integration.

After lengthy debate and compromise, Congress approved a plan with court enforcement and without OFCC transfer in 1972. The opposition of organized labor had been neutralized by expanding EEOC jurisdiction, and in addition the EEOC gained authority to move against "patterns or practices" of discrimination from the Justice Department. With its expanded powers, the EEOC rapidly found itself in trouble, however. By the end of fiscal 1974 it had a case backlog of 97,761 cases, with 70,000 new cases expected in fiscal 1975 and 85,000 more in fiscal 1976. Another round of procedural changes seemed necessary if EEOC was to carry out its obligations effectively.

Issues Seek Their Own Level

The American system of federal sharing of powers among local, state, and national governments often leads to jurisdictional conflict, especially when policies themselves are controversial. Perhaps just as often, federal sharing of powers turns into federal passing of the buck, when politicians at one level seek to rid themselves of a problematic issue by passing it up, or down, to another level in the system. Usually this can be done with little difficulty because the boundaries of local, state, and national responsibilities are customarily set only by bargaining or adjudication of disputes over existing programs.[11] The responsibility for unresolved issues may well reside nowhere in particular.

Interest groups seeking access at one level of government "know" they are getting a runaround when they are told the important decisions about the program of interest to them are made somewhere else. But if the same group could mount political strength at more than one level, it might find the federal system a blessing. Multiplication of competent, quasi-autonomous governmental units provides alternate access points for issue publics organized to take advantage of them. Problems arise for groups unable to act effectively at more than one level. State politicians, for example, will often be less eager to respond if they see that a problem has been dealt with nationally, and they have successfully pushed the problem onto local governments. So an apparent nonresponse may exist in the minds of a claimant group, but the possibility of response at another level in the federal system makes the whole question moot.

The growing volume of social science research on the adoption of innovations by American state governments, far from giving a definite answer to this question, reflects the same ambiguity. In some instances, national government action preempts a field of concern even before the states have acted; in others, nearly every state has responded to a social issue by the time any federal action is taken. For some issues, response at both state and federal levels awaits a crucial court test; for others, federal and state officials engage in running conflict over a long span of time, and no clear winner emerges.

The field of labor legislation provides fascinating examples of federal-state interaction that, collectively, demonstrate the complexity of the federalism effect.[12] Laws requiring employers to compensate employees for work-related injuries, for example, show a pattern of federal initiative voluntarily taken up by the

---

[11] For illustrations of this proposition, see Daniel J. Elazar, *American Federalism: A View From the States*, New York, Thomas Y. Crowell Company, 1966.

[12] U.S. Department of Labor, *Growth of Labor Law in the United States*, Washington, Government Printing Office, 1967.

individual states. During the early 1900s there was considerable state interest in workmen's compensation legislation, and one law was passed in Maryland in 1902, but declared unconstitutional. The federal legislation of 1908 was the first workmen's compensation law to pass the constitutionality test. Three more state laws were declared unconstitutional, in 1909, 1910, and 1914, but thereafter all enactments proved acceptable to the courts. The first successful state enactments came in 1911, and within 10 years 44 states, Puerto Rico, and the District of Columbia had passed similar laws. The last state to join the list, Mississippi, passed its law in 1948.

Labor relations legislation, similar to the Wagner Act (1935) or Taft-Hartley Act (1947), illustrates federal preemption. The Wagner Act, declaring unions' rights to organize and bargain collectively, applied solely to interstate commerce. To remedy this deficiency, 12 states and Puerto Rico passed similar legislation between 1935 and 1947. Following the passage of Taft-Hartley, only one state has put its own labor relations act into effect. The increasingly interstate character of all economic activity, the more generous court interpretation of the meaning of "interstate commerce," and the more anti-union tone of the Taft-Hartley and Landrum-Griffin (1959) acts all made further state action in this area irrelevant.

The so-called "right to work" laws show the potential importance of federal preemption in a manner exactly opposite to the labor relations laws. Here, the states deferred to federal law until the law itself was changed to clarify the extent of state prerogative. Following the passage of the Wagner Act in 1935, and its judicial acceptance two years later, states were reluctant to infringe the newly won rights of labor unions. Toward the end of World War II, however, with labor militancy rising again, five states did attempt to declare right-to-work policies. All five chose the route of constitutional amendment, probably feeling that they might thereby avoid the problem of unconstitutionality. The same union militancy against which the states acted also led to the Taft-Hartley Act in 1947. Section 14(b) of that act allowed states individually to outlaw union shop arrangements, although Taft-Hartley itself permits the union shop subject to certain conditions, outlawing only the closed shop. Responding to this new freedom to legislate, 17 states passed right-to-work laws, while only two (including one of the 17) used the constitutional amendment procedure to the same effect. Eleven of the 17 states taking advantage of their new 14(b) freedom did so the same year Taft-Hartley was passed, clearly showing that prior to 1947 they had been discouraged by federal action.

The long and tortuous history of national fair employment practice law has been summarized in a previous section. Similar actions at the state level reveal two significant patterns: (1) a number of states responded to pleas for antidiscrimination laws before Congress did, and (2) another group of states, almost as numerous, followed the federal lead closely. The period 1945 to 1965 conveniently demarcates the dramatic rise of the American civil rights movement. The first date marks the initial peacetime steps toward equal rights in federal employment; the second, in the Voting Rights Act of 1965, marks a firm national commitment to equal access to the ballot. In the two intervening decades, the armed services and public facilities were desegregated, school desegregation was begun, and the poll tax was abolished. During this period, both state and national governments felt the urgency of civil rights demands, in employment and in other areas. Puerto Rico and 25 states passed fair employment practice acts between 1945 and 1964, before any sort of federal legislative success was achieved. In the two years following the creation of the EEOC in 1964, another 11 states passed their own antidiscrimination laws.

One final instance of federal sharing in labor law, that of minimum wage laws, also shows both independent state adoptions and state adoptions directly stimulated by federal action.[13] In the Progressive period—roughly the first two decades of this century—14 states, Puerto Rico, and the District of Columbia adopted minimum wage laws. Many of these came to grief in the 1920s, however, as federal and state courts came into the hands of strict constructionists and business-oriented jurists. The New

[13] Robert Eyestone, "Confusion, Diffusion and Innovation," *American Political Science Review*, **71** (1977), pp. 445–6.

Deal period of the 1930s produced both federal minimum wage legislation and new state enactments, but the state laws came first. A total of 17 states added such laws between 1933 and 1937, while the federal Fair Labor Standards Act was not passed until 1938. When it did finally appear, the federal law was more comprehensive than the earlier state enactments, and at least 10 states upgraded their laws after 1938 to conform to the federal legislation.

Careful readers may have noticed that these examples don't really show issues seeking their own levels. In the area of labor legislation, certainly, very similar issues rose to prominence simultaneously at the national level and in many states. In some metaphoric sense, though, issue responses do emerge at the level where political forces are most favorable to them. The evidence of policy diffusions often shows the unresponsiveness of the national government, in contrast to some states. But it is only *some* states that are so progressive. Beyond question, there is more difference between the state ranked No. 1 on any policy scale and the state ranked No. 50, than there is between the country as a whole and either of these extremes. The great variability among states is reflected in their politics, and their politics in turn produce great variability in policy responsiveness.

State diversity is not really much help to issue claimants; at best, it may have a kind of exemplary force, as the policy diffusion studies have found.[14] National labor unions may rejoice at the passage of state minimum wage laws, for example, but a Minnesota law is of little benefit to a worker in New Jersey. The force of example may be important, but it must also be strongly conditioned by local political factors. Thus New Jersey will have a minimum wage law when it is politically ready to have one, even though it may adopt the Minnesota law word for word when the time comes. In the meantime, New Jersey unions must

---

[14] Eyestone, "Confusion, Diffusion and Innovation"; Virginia Gray, "Innovation in the States: A Diffusion Study," *American Political Science Review*, **67** (1973), pp. 1174–85; Jack L. Walker, "The Diffusion of Innovations Among the American States," *American Political Science Review*, **63** (1969), pp. 880–99.

be frustrated in their efforts, perhaps doubly so in that they have the model law in hand, ready for emulation when the time is right for it.

Why Many issues Seem to Be Ignored

The examples presented in this chapter show that many issues may seem to be ignored because the expectations of one or more groups pressing for a change in policy have been frustrated. Their expectations can be unreasonable in one of five ways:

1. They expect action not merely a decision.
2. They expect an all-out commitment instead of a token or pilot effort.
3. They expect predictability from policy responses.
4. They expect an immediate response.
5. They expect that the issue can be resolved everywhere if it has gotten a response anywhere.

As detached observers, we know that these expectations will often be disappointed because we can see the pitfalls and imperfections in the issue translation process. Unfortunately, this kind of general staff knowledge does not help the front line troops get on with the business at hand—winning some sort of issue response in the face of difficulties they may know little about.

For group strategies, the conclusion must be that it is not unreasonable to act on unreasonable expectations. The rational course of action for an issue public is to press its demands without worrying whether they are unreasonable in some abstract sense, because this is certainly the best way to test the practicality of their demands. If civil rights groups had not persevered in their efforts to get fair employment legislation, if unions had not continued to test the judicial acceptability of pro-union policies, if pro-life and pro-abortion groups now give up the struggle, these issues would be resolved in less satisfactory fashion if at all. The record for the big spending programs—housing programs and education aid, for example—is less optimistic, but the difficulty there comes from uncertainty about the appropriate policy response (see Chapter 3). This problem will be considered again after a look at some examples of truly ignored issues, in the next chapter.

7

Why Some Issues Are Ignored

Important issues are often ignored for long periods, long enough to require strategies different from those appropriate to more routine issues. The cause of inaction is usually political, involving either the resistance of an overt power structure or the powerlessness of an issue public. *Effective* responses to issues require a conjunction of governmental information, governmental capacity, and political will. Only the last of these three is necessary for a response that is less than effective, however, and if politics is also stacked against an issue claimant, it can easonably expect no response at all. Just how this process works can best be shown by example.

Vague Demands, Trivial Issues

Several excuses for nonresponse are perennial favorites with politicians, and among these the notion of trivial demands is prominent. When an issue public makes a consistent demand, and is rebuffed at every turn by political institutions with the power to respond to the demand, the issue public may naturally claim that a "power elite" is frustrating the popular will. Often there is no easy way to identify a power elite, and unless we are prepared to plot a revolution there may be little consolation in knowing that our oppressor is a distinct power elite instead of that anonymous villain, "politics as usual." However, the existence of power elites can sometimes be inferred because they contradict the pluralist assumptions that are commonly thought to apply to American politics. Ordinarily we would expect politics to be open and fluid, with a multiplicity of groups competing among themselves on a basis of approximate equality in political resources.[1] If governmental institutions appear instead to be monolithic, and if a few groups dominate all others by their superior command of political resources, a power elite is present.

The thwarted efforts of consumer advocates to have their own consumer protection agency provide an example of a power elite associated with business dominance of the government apparatus. Bills to create such an agency date back to 1959. Both President Kennedy and President Johnson sent consumer messages to Congress, but little further action was taken until 1969. Consumer groups and Democratic congressmen criticized President Nixon early in his first term for making no consumer statement and for failing to fill several important consumer posts in the government. They were, consequently, very skeptical about the sincerity of the Nixon administration's commitment to the consumer area when a consumer message, issued late in 1969, proposed expanding the Office of Consumer Affairs in the White House and increasing the Justice Department's efforts on the consumer's behalf, rather than creating a new Cabinet level Department.

Concerns for the sincerity of presidential commitment were given a boost when Nixon threatened to veto any bill that contained plans for Justice Department lawyers to act as advocates for aggrieved consumers when those consumers brought their case before other government agencies. In late 1972, business lobbies working with the administration managed to defeat a cloture motion in the Senate that would have brought a House-

---

[1] Michael Parenti, "Power and Pluralism: A View from the Bottom," *Journal of Politics*, **32** (1970), pp. 501–30. See also Kenneth Prewitt and Alan Stone, *The Ruling Elites: Elite Theory, Power, and American Democracy*, New York, Harper and Row, 1973.

approved consumer agency bill to the floor. The stalemate continued after the 1972 elections, with Congress passing bills for a Consumer Protection Agency, and Presidents Nixon and Ford threatening to veto them.

The rationale offered for a consumer protection agency was that it would coordinate the multifarious federal programs affecting consumers, conduct and disseminate research and product testing information, and represent consumers in court cases arising over the reliability or safety of products and services. Critics argued that this was a vague and overly ambitious effort, that it represented undue interference in the management of private enterprise, and that it was unnecessary because it passed over the existing consumer agencies such as the Federal Trade Commission. Besides being vague, consumer demands were labeled as trivial because they sought a mechanism that was unnecessary and would not be effective.

A variety of inferences could be drawn from this brief illustration, but the most persuasive explanation is simply that Presidents Nixon and Ford, acting for the interests of American business, organized a kind of monolithic opposition against more liberal consumer protection demands. The justifications offered for this resistance were largely that, justifications, designed to soften the blow when the "power elite" ultimately did succeed in preventing action. The intention of this example, and the following one, is to show that power elites need not be indistinct figures lurking in the Washington shadows. There are real world equivalents for the shadowy image—Wall Street tycoons, perhaps, foreign agents, military contractors, and even religious leaders—but explanations for the fate of public issues need not look so far afield. For present purposes, power elites are neither more nor less than dominant political groups.

Issues Not for Governments to Handle

A nonresponse particularly hard to counter is the claim that an issue is inappropriate for government action. Here, again, a power elite can be inferred if a consistent and overt bias appears in all political institutions. When any single government agency shunts an issue aside with this excuse, it can safely be assumed that the agency means merely that *it* is powerless to respond effectively. However, when the same excuse is used consistently, then a universal prejudice of some sort is present.

The boundaries between American government and non-government (whether economic or social) are well maintained, and only a small number of issues seriously pose a question of government involvement. Some aspects of the slavery question dealt with the legitimate exercise of government power, for example, but the attempted nullification of national policy by state actions in the South, and the extension of slavery to new territories soon to be admitted as states, inevitably brought the national government into this issue. Similarly, it might have seemed during the 1920s that federal courts were attempting to recreate the philosophy of laissez faire in economic regulation, but the inventiveness of the states during this period revealed the essentially federal/constitutional nature of this essay in judicial assertion.

The boundary between church and state has been settled for a long time. Is there any evidence that school prayer and parochial school aid invoke the question of a legitimate governmental role? School prayer controversies usually deal with the question, "what is religion?" The efforts of local school districts to dilute the religious formula students are asked to recite, to secure court acceptance of the formula, show the districts' orientations to be pietistic rather than sectarian.[2] The U.S. Supreme Court has undoubtedly gone beyond the intentions of the writers of the Bill of Rights, who denied Congress the power to legislate regarding an establishment of religion. Having few non-Christians in their constituencies, the Founding Fathers were little concerned with the rights of atheists—it was the sectarian strife in England, palely reflected among the colonies, they sought to avoid. The paradox of the Court's action is that, in bending over backward to avoid sectarian bias, the justices have become

---

[2] Kenneth M. Dolbeare and Phillip E. Hammond, *The School Prayer Decisions,* Chicago, University of Chicago Press, 1971.

deeply involved, albeit unwillingly, in defining religion itself.

Sex discrimination qualifies as an issue on the public-private boundary, if only because pleas for a definite federal statement on the subject went unheeded for more than 25 years. None of the three federal branches responded for more than four decades following ratification of the female suffrage amendment in 1923, and the record of the states is little better. On the prima facie evidence, then, the denial of government responsibility for women's rights (except voting) reflects a grand sexist conspiracy. A closer look at the events leading up to the Equal Rights Amendment will help to test and refine this explanation.

Bills for some kind of equal rights statement were introduced in Congress every year since 1923, but they never got very far until the middle 1960s. The Senate Judiciary Committee reported favorably on the bills a number of times, but the two times they received a favorable vote in the Senate (1950 and 1953) they included an amendment exempting legal forms of discrimination, thereby vitiating the effect of the bills. There was no significant federal action on women's rights in government employment until 1967, when the nondiscrimination rules were extended to sex by executive order. An executive order in 1965 had required each federal agency to establish its own equal employment program, and the Civil Service Commission began an effort to include women in these programs in 1968. Also in 1968 and 1969, the EEOC attempted to break the customary pattern of male dominance in many jobs by issuing guidelines restricting the identification of sex qualifications in classified newspaper advertisements.

The House of Representatives acted first in 1970, passing an equal rights amendment after successfully discharging the House Judiciary Committee of responsibility for the bill. The amendment was strongly opposed by the committee's chairman, Emanuel Celler (D–N.Y.) because he felt it would destroy essential protective legislation based on inherent physical, emotional, and psychological differences between men and women. Senate leadership placed the House-passed amendment directly on the calendar, bypassing the Senate Judiciary Committee and chairman Sam Ervin (D–N.C.), who also strongly opposed the bill, but action was not completed that year or the next. Some of the momentum of equal rights was lost in 1971 when the Supreme Court for the first time overturned a state law on grounds of arbitrary sex discrimination. Since the sponsors of the Equal Rights Amendment had argued that judicial failure to act on sex discrimination necessitated the amendment, the court's action threw the continuing need for ERA into question.

ERA was finally sent to the states for ratification early in 1972, after the Senate voted down a long series of weakening amendments proposed by Senator Ervin. Within a year, 28 states had ratified it and 12 had voted against it, leaving ERA's fate uncertain. A period of seven years for ratification was allowed, so its opponents need to hold out only until 1979 to defeat the amendment.

Until the middle 1960s, sex discrimination had been a hands-off question for the federal government. Policy changes in all three branches of government between 1967 and 1971, described above, suggest by their close timing that some forces external to government brought about the new responsiveness, and that response had been prevented prior to the middle 1960s by a sort of power elite, or in this case a sexist conspiracy. The women's liberation movement must rate high among the external forces enhancing responsiveness to equal rights demands, but in addition, the social and economic changes on which the women's liberation movement is based probably also had a direct impact on politics. Increasing educational attainment among women, more women workers, declining family size, increasing divorce rate—these factors all would have entered the consciousness of politicians and perhaps disposed them more favorably to an Equal Rights Amendment. A majority of states quickly added their approval to the two-thirds majority in both houses of Congress, but the extraordinary majority of three-fourths of the states required to ratify the Constitution casts some doubt on the thoroughness of the women's revolution. Only 13 of the smaller, less urbanized states in the union need to vote against the amendment, or merely fail to vote for it, and it will not be adopted.

Politics as Usual

"Politics as usual" implies a wide range of political phenomena, all perfectly normal, legal, and open, and all capable of derailing the issue translation process at any of a number of points. Issues may be prejudiced from the beginning because some parties to the issue conflict lack political resources such as size, money, or political skills. The political process seems inherently biased against some issues, even when it is not monolithic. In other instances, previous government decisions create bureaucracies that resist policy change even in the face of changed external circumstances. Finally, some issues are in the public eye too short a time—they are displaced before they can receive any significant response.

"Politics as usual" pervades all the reasons so far cited for apparent and real response failure. For instance, the groups bargaining over the terms of an issue resolution may be of greatly unequal weight. If one group has built up a substantial range of contacts within government agencies, and the smaller or newer one is on its own, it almost certainly will come out second in the eventual dividing up of the rewards. Another instance—the gestation periods of issues like racial discrimination are not really inevitable. A so-called gestation period is simply a time of waiting for social and economic changes to overcome the initial political disadvantage under which the claimant public is laboring. Thus the creation of an Equal Employment Opportunity Commission in 1964 was achieved as part of a large civil rights coalition of blacks and white liberals. The addition of enforcement powers had to wait another eight years while sources of opposition within government were worn down and enough experience was gained under the 1964 act to calm the worst fears of the opponents of enforcement powers.

In this chapter, the notion of "politics as usual" denotes several specific political phenomena in the issue translation process. The first of these is the shortage of group resources or political experience. At the extreme, a group may be essentially unorganized and inarticulate, and its requests may find their way to governmental agencies only indirectly. The importance of political entrepreneurs in channeling issues to governmental agencies was described in Chapter 5. Entrepreneurs *do* perform this valuable service, but not for everyone and not without bias. Some issues are ignored because the groups seeking to bring them to public attention lack the political resources either to put their issue on a governmental agenda directly or to enlist the aid of entrepreneurs to publicize the issue for them.

How could it be that any group of people in the United States, having a point of view on a significant issue, cannot muster the minimal level of organizational strength needed to gain exposure in American politics? One problem is that some supposed issues do not really meet the terms of the definition advanced in Chapter 1; most often, they do not display the requisite level of public disagreement about solutions. For instance, there have been sporadic attempts since 1913, when the sixteenth amendment to the constitution was ratified, to abolish the income tax. The very small group of people of this persuasion—indeed, isolated individuals—attempt to argue that income taxation is a deprivation of property contrary to the fourteenth amendment, even though the sixteenth amendment makes their argument untenable in the courts.

A somewhat more significant version of the same argument is the case brought by single persons against the income tax laws. They complain that the tax rate schedules discriminate against single persons in favor of married couples. For their part, married working couples claim that the tax laws discriminate against them, and some contemplate "tax divorces" as a sophisticated form of tax avoidance. The phenomenon of "Social Security sin," where cohabiting couples over 65 remain unmarried to avoid reduction in their Social Security benefits, is prompted by a similar motivation. Principles of abstract justice probably have little to do with these issues, for one never hears one-worker families complaining that the laws discriminate in their favor, and homeowners do not object to the deductibility of their mortgage interest payments. Equity breaks are always fair to those who receive them.

The point of these examples, with their superficial similarities as public issues, is that there is a wide variation in the ability of the various groups involved to bring their point of view before tax policy makers. The few people still questioning the constitutionality of the income tax system must raise their arguments through individual court cases, and they have no chance of getting assistance from any organized taxpayers or civil rights groups, such as the American Civil Liberties Union, because everyone else believes the issue to have been settled long ago. The singles have a better chance of expressing their point of view effectively, even if there is little chance that they can get much satisfaction from the IRS or the courts. There are substantial numbers of single taxpayers, and their numbers and the extent of their financial sacrifice under the tax laws can be estimated from readily available statistics of tax returns. But the recent restrictions on class action legal suits make it virtually impossible for an individual taxpayer to carry forward a class action suit, and the relatively small personal cost of tax law discrimination makes it unlikely that any individual taxpayer would take on the IRS single-handed. Unless some interest group, already involved with questions of tax equity, is attracted to the case, little is likely to come of it.

Between 1966, when Congress revised and approved procedures for federal class action suits, and 1974, when a Supreme Court ruling greatly limited their use, class action suits had been a favored method for consumers and environmentalists to join their individually small stakes in a particular case into a potent legal force. Aided by sympathetic courts and liberal interpretations of the 1966 guidelines, groups with a relatively small organizational base initiated suits on behalf of much larger unorganized groups of citizens.

In the case that brought the 1974 ruling, for instance, a plaintiff with a $70 stake in odd lot stock brokers fees would technically have been required to bear the $225,000 cost of notifying the two million members of his class before his suit could proceed. A federal district court ruled first that notification of a sample of this class, at a cost of only $22,000, would meet the procedural requirements. It then determined that there was a good chance the plaintiff would win the case, and ordered the brokerage firms cited as defendents in the case to pay 90% of the costs of notification. The appeals court and then the Supreme Court overturned this decision, reimposing the requirement that the plaintiff must pay the full cost of informing all members of the class before the suit could go forward. In a related ruling the previous year, the Supreme Court declared that class action suits where no federal question was involved could be brought in federal court only if each member of the class had a claim of $10,000 or more.

Of the issue publics just described, only the over-65s would now have much chance of winning their case against the Social Security system. They are an identifiable class, as the singles are, and the extent of their individual stake is also readily measurable. In addition, they are represented by effective lobby groups such as the American Association of Retired People, and they function more clearly as a reference group for their members, especially in retirement communities, sun cities, and high rise housing for the aged built under federal housing programs. The AARP can lobby Congress to change the Social Security laws, or even organize a class action suit for its members if this seemed like a good strategy. The single taxpayers and the married working couples, without any of these social or political advantages, are severely handicapped in bringing similar complaints before policy makers.

The handgun control issue, an emotion-laden perennial among the "social regulation" questions, exemplifies some additional features of "politics as usual." To begin with, handgun control is just a facet of the long-standing social debate over firearms and personal weapons of all kinds. The issue cannot be defined as handgun control alone, because the emotional overtones of the debate quickly involve the groups on both sides concerned about guns of any kind. The oldest and largest pro-gun lobby, the National Rifle Association, chooses to emphasize its safety programs, concern for legitimate sporting use of weapons, and marksmanship, yet it has been the most effective spokesman on the regulation of Saturday night specials, the small, cheap guns often used in street crime and generally conceded to be useless for safe sport or accurate target shooting.

The emotional attachment to firearms on the one side, and

the elemental fear of crime by core city residents on the other side, lead to the most hyperbolic statements of the issue that the two sides can put forward. Gun control is held to violate the Second Amendment right to keep and bear arms, as if the constitutionally identified need for a militia meant that everyone could have a cheap handgun under the pillow. The slogan "When guns are outlawed, only outlaws will have guns" joins two misleading arguments. First, law enforcement officials would also have guns. Second, the most prominent proposals to control guns have advocated registration, not prohibition, and those proposals that did contemplate prohibition did not refer to all guns, or even to all handguns, but only to all nonsporting handguns of a certain size, construction, and so on.

The neat distinction between criminals and "law-abiding citizens," intended to appeal to big city residents worried about violent crime, overlooks the injury and death caused by otherwise law-abiding citizens who—just once—reach impulsively for a gun to settle a barroom quarrel or family dispute. The states rights argument is also heard from time to time, when opponents of gun control attack federal regulation by asserting that the problem should be handled locally, and in response to local needs.

Although national majorities have consistently supported handgun control, significant advances in gun control legislation have occurred only in the face of national emergencies or crimes that have shocked the national conscience. Federal laws in the 1930s were passed in response to gangland crime and an assassination attempt on President Roosevelt. The handgun control section of the Omnibus Crime Control and Safe Streets Act of 1968 was passed as a direct result of the assassinations of Robert Kennedy and Martin Luther King. The Senate passed a strengthened handgun control bill in 1972 after Senator John Stennis was robbed and shot on the streets of Washington.

Why is it that the proponents of gun control are so ineffective politically? One reason gun control has not gone forward more rapidly is that its opponents enjoy superior organization. They can contact their constituency easily, first through sporting magazines and then through NRA membership rolls. There is no correspondingly easy way to find and sign up supporters of gun control. It is the old problem of organizing diffuse interests—very few people among the mulititude favoring stronger control can be persuaded to work or pay for effective lobbying, because they hope that someone else who feels more strongly on the issue will carry the burden of advocating it.[3] Gun ownership is a private good (although susceptible to justification in public terms), while gun control is a public good (but requires private resource expenditures to achieve).

In the absence of a well-organized control lobby, many interest groups have taken a stand on gun control even though the issue was incidental to their essential organizational focus. Civil rights groups, women's groups, unions, and religious groups have all—temporarily—found a common thread in their opposition to violence, but their efforts have been frustrated because politicians realize that the level of involvement of these groups, as groups, with the gun control issue is low and sporadic. The great advantage enjoyed by the gun lobby is its ability to stimulate massive mailings against gun control at critical stages in legislative consideration of gun control proposals. In the absence of regularly organized control lobbies, only the drama of gangland crimes and assassinations of major public figures will generate the spontaneous outpouring of public feeling that can convince legislators they can safely vote for more stringent control.

Lobby groups favoring gun control do exist, and their organizational problems only serve to underscore the "politics as usual" explanation for our gun control laws. The National Council for a Responsible Firearms Policy, with about 2000 members (compared with NRA's million plus) was founded in 1967. Its Executive Director is also the Executive Director of the Committee for a National Trade Policy, a loosely organized free trade group. Prominent on the NCRFP's board are former prison officials, former Treasury agents, former big city mayors, and pacifists of various sorts. The general image of the council is of a group formed out of vague liberal frustrations with urban

---

[3] This argument has been put forward most clearly by Mancur Olson, Jr., *The Logic of Collective Action*, Cambridge, Harvard University Press, 1965.

violence, cultivating a rather small and diverse coalition of interest groups that may be similarly frustrated from time to time, but would otherwise lack any effective way of pressing their demands in Washington. A membership of 2000 will not keep a shoestring enterprise like NCRFP afloat indefinitely, and the dry spells must be dry indeed. This, in a nutshell, is "politics as usual."

Critics of American pluralist democracy sometimes put the shoe on the other foot, arguing not that some interests are unorganized but that politicians are prejudiced against certain kinds of demands. The two competing arguments are hard to disentangle, because the motives of elected politicians are similar in the two cases. The failure to close tax loopholes, for example, is often brought forward as an illustration of congressional bias. Legislators are dependent on business campaign contributions, the argument goes, and they therefore will not vote against tax favors for business interests. The business background of many legislators, either directly or as small town lawyers, is cited as further evidence of a business bias in Congress.

The same arguments could be made to explain the failure of strict gun control legislation. Legislators are fearful of the wrath of the gun lobby because it can sway the votes of many sportsmen, and perhaps also their financial support. At the same time, congressmen are "gun conscious" in other ways as well. Most of them are veterans of military service, and many are themselves sportsmen. Representatives from western and rural areas, and nearly all Senators, have substantial gun-owning constituencies and also personal backgrounds that would dispose them to gun owners. So it may be meaningless to try to decide whether a politician is personally biased in favor of one side of an issue, or is merely being forced for electoral reasons to go along with their viewpoint, because the same behavior results whatever the explanation may be. This, too, is "politics as usual."

Entrenched bureaucratic interests exemplify a final variety of politics as usual. In policy areas where some governmental response has occurred, the critical political structure is an informal subgovernment, formed of congressional committee members and staff, bureaucrats, and private group organizations relevant to the issue area in question.[4] Subgovernments are not generally important because they administer massive programs that affect large numbers of people. Instead, their significance for the social issue process is largely potential, resting on their ability to defend established privilege against outside efforts to adopt new public-oriented policies, and manifesting itself only when the interests of the subgovernment members are challenged.

The bureaucracy itself is usually the moving force that maintains the subgovernment's influence. Francis E. Rourke observes that neutral bureaucracies are impossible in a system such as ours, where political parties fail to perform the functions of program development and the mobilization of political support.[5] Executive agencies must carry out these tasks for themselves, relying primarily on a favorable public image and specific support from attentive publics. Skillful agencies can act as their own lobby, or better yet they can organize outside pressures to which they can appear to be responding.[6]

Subgovernments dominate the issue translation process through their control of external group access to governmental decision making channels. In a study conducted in the late 1960s, for example, Harold Wolman found that access to housing elites was greatest for those groups favoring the Johnson administration's policy, and least for the planners and black groups seeking the greatest policy change.[7] Wolman interprets these findings as evidence of a failure of effective communication by the most radical groups, but the data are also perfectly consistent with a "discouragement" hypothesis—change-oriented groups did not work very hard to put their views across because they expected little sympathy from the housing elites.

[4] See generally Randall B. Ripley and Grace A. Franklin, *Congress, The Bureaucracy, and Public Policy,* Homewood, Ill., The Dorsey Press, 1976.

[5] Francis E. Rourke, *Bureaucracy, Politics, and Public Policy,* Boston, Little, Brown and Company, 1969, p. 12.

[6] J. Leiper Freeman, "The Bureaucracy in Pressure Politics," *Annals of the American Academy of Political and Social Science,* **319** (1958), pp. 10–19.

[7] Harold Wolman, *The Politics of Federal Housing,* New York, Dodd, Mead and Company, 1971, pp. 60–69.

Under appropriate circumstances, most notably shifts in national political party fortunes, presidential appointment powers may be used to reorient a subgovernment even without any formal shift in legislative policy. Seymour Harris writes about the phenomenon he calls "repeal by appointment," where the Eisenhower administration brought about major shifts in public housing, foreign aid, public power, and other policy areas simply by adroit use of the appointment power.[8] Outgoing administrations seek to prevent such change by filling all vacancies themselves and making program commitments as far ahead as possible.[9]

Policy changes made in this way could be considered as evidence for a kind of governmental responsiveness, but the process is neither open nor public. Response is the result of accommodations between governmental and private elite groups, and whether the public perspective is adequately represented may be seriously questioned.

Displaced Issues

A final, very common reason for issues being ignored is issue displacement. Because of the peculiarities of the public agenda described in Chapter 4, issues are frequently displaced before they achieve a definitive resolution. When one issue pushes another off the public agenda, the impetus to action is cut short all along the line. Public pressure is reduced when the issue is taken from public view, and issue entrepreneurs shift their efforts (if possible) to where the action is. Politicians and government bureaucrats, for their part, will also readjust their action priorities to coincide with the new focus of public interest, since a large part of the political game is showing concern for the right problems even if you cannot do anything substantial about them.

Certain types of issues on the public agenda tend to be dis-

[8] Quoted in Louis C. Gawthrop, *Bureaucratic Behavior in the Executive Branch: An Analysis of Organizational Change,* New York, The Free Press, 1969, p. 62.
[9] Monroe W. Karmin, "Locking Nixon In," *Wall Street Journal,* November 22, 1968.

placed quite rapidly, as shown in Chapter 4, whether they have been resolved or not, while other issues remain on the public agenda, at a lower level of urgency, even though they are resolved gradually in piecemeal fashion. Shifts in the public agenda are transmitted to politicians rapidly, but they do not always change official agendas as rapidly. A few politicians, at any rate, take seriously their commitment to respond to issues on which they have made a pledge of responsiveness, and a handful, especially those in leadership positions, may attempt to do this even though the terrain has shifted under them. The results often reveal some of the basic political dimensions of the issue translation process.

The energy crisis of 1973–74 exemplifies an externally generated problem that rose rapidly on the public agenda and then fell again almost as quickly. The shortfall of domestic oil production relative to demand had been growing gradually in the early 1970s, and President Nixon lifted the oil import quota in April 1973 to increase the supply available for sale in the United States. The OPEC oil embargo and the fourfold increase in crude oil prices begun in October 1973 prompted a dramatic reversal in policy, including a number of oil conservation measures and the launching of Project Independence, a grab-bag of executive proposals to increase domestic supply, limit and manage domestic demand, and reduce reliance on foreign energy sources. These were only short-term measures, however, and it fell to Congress to draft a coherent long-range policy on energy.

Congress and the White House bickered over energy policy all through 1974 and 1975, with each castigating the other for failing to produce a comprehensive long-range energy management policy. President Ford kept pressure on Congress by periodically proposing to increase oil import duties to hold down demand and stimulate domestic production, and Congress was forced to vote these down or compromise with Ford to buy time to put together its own energy policy. After months of work, the House Ways and Means Committee finally sent to the floor an energy conservation bill based largely on tax incentives and tax penalties. The bill was unpopular in the committee, being reported out by an unenthusiastic 19 to 16 vote, and the House first delayed action and then voted against the committee plan by a lopsided vote of 345 to 72.

Where had the energy crisis gone? Legislators must have wondered the same thing when they checked with their constituents early in 1975 and found no sentiment for higher taxes for energy or anything else. It turned out that the public never really saw an energy crisis. They did indeed see a gasoline shortage, and some few saw a heating oil shortage, but as these dislocations eased in late 1974, and did not recur in the mild winter of 1975, the impetus for an energy policy virtually disappeared. Members of Congress had been pushed out on a limb in trying to respond conscientiously to an energy crisis, but they had the misfortune to bring in their proposals after the crisis had passed.

The failure to adopt an energy policy promptly is not all that serious if one is not needed immediately, and if this were the only effect issue displacement has, there would be little cause for concern. Issue displacement may have more lasting effects when it is translated into governmental prejudice. For instance, several features of Project Independence finally voted into law in a compromise bill enacted at the end of 1975 seem to buy energy independence at considerable cost to the environment. The act gave the president authority to require maximum production from oil and gas wells, pushed back the date for air pollution compliance by power plants so that they could burn more high sulphur coal, and opened up oil reserves to exploitation. Approval of the Alaskan oil pipeline and presidential vetoes of bills regulating strip mining also exemplify the tradeoff of environmental protection for energy production made politically possible by the displacement of the environmental issue by the energy crisis.

In addition to being a "natural" occurrence, issue displacement may be a conscious political strategy as well. President Ford was very successful, in his first few months in office, in displacing the unemployment issue with the inflation issue, and then in redefining the inflation issue along lines more suitable for a Republican administration. The WIN program (Whip Inflation Now) and the economic summit meetings held in late 1974 were not terribly significant as sources of new ideas on the inflation problem, but they were highly effective in shifting both unemployment and inflation off the president's shoulders. Both these efforts strongly implied that the government had done all it could to fight inflation, and that the fight must now be taken up by individual citizens. Both also greatly raised the visibility of the inflation problem, from a "most important problem" rating of 48% in June 1974, to a rating of 81 percent in October. Unfortunately for the administration, all this effort did not change popular opinions about which party could handle the country's problems better; the Democrats continued to enjoy a 2-to-1 advantage, with almost half of all respondents thinking neither party was superior.

It should be clear that politics is central to all these examples of how issues can be ignored. Whether the barrier to effective response is lack of political power on the part of issue publics or prejudice on the part of politicians may in the long run make little difference because the results are generally the same. The next chapter examines the possibility that certain kinds of political circumstances, beyond the control of either publics or politicians, may create conditions favorable for successful issue translation.

8

Response in Normality and Crisis

Crisis and Impermanence

Commentators and political scientists have long recognized the relationship of crisis to the speed of governmental actions, although an understanding of the dynamics and causes of political crisis has been more elusive. A crisis is usually described as a situation, caused by external forces, in which definite and prompt action is necessary. In practice this definition is often tautological, because a need for action can be identified only by observing shared feelings of crisis among decision makers and the public at large.

The feeling that action is necessary comes from a weighing of the expected gains from acting against the probable costs from failure to act. Consequences of a failure to act so far outweigh the feared costs or unknown results of acting, that the normal political resistance and delay is swept aside. The popular idea of timely action to avert a crisis usually means avoiding the consequences of a failure to act, instead of avoiding the crisis and the necessity to decide.

A political crisis is not the same as an opportunity, and the response to the two differs in predictable fashion. In both, the political calculations revolve around the benefits of action and the costs of inaction, but the main cost of failing to take an opportunity is the foregone benefit of the opportunity itself, as

153

discussed in Chapter 4. In a crisis it is largely the costs of failing to act that compel a response, whether there are additional benefits to be gained or not. Thus a crisis action coalition may contain a large number of people who seek merely to "avert" the crisis and who do not necessarily look forward to any positive benefit from its successful resolution. Failure to take up opportunities may also be thought to involve costs, but these are mostly the foregone benefits of the opportunity itself. Arguments invoking the potential loss of these benefits will be persuasive only to people who already favor the benefits in a positive sense, consequently action coalitions for taking political opportunities will contain only direct supporters of such opportunities. Thus coalitions pursuing political opportunities are more closely related to their ultimate goal but less likely to succeed because of their smaller size; crisis-oriented coalitions are less closely linked to their end goals but are larger and therefore more likely to succeed.

As an illustration of this somewhat paradoxical point, consider the general strategy for urban problems in the 1960s. The passage of civil rights legislation, especially the 1964 and 1965 bills, the aid to education legislation of 1965, the tax cut of 1964, and the Model Cities program together should have created the opportunity for a more comprehensive urban strategy because these individual measures brought together a loose urban-based coalition that would support further innovation. But the relatively small number of politicians who attempted to go further in the solution of urban problems could not muster the numbers or sense of urgency required. When riots erupted in many of the cities thought to be benefiting the most from existing policy measures, a much broader coalition called for a law and order response that was considerably less beneficial for the solution of urban problems than other approaches that might have been chosen.

The sense of the politically possible is a crucial determinant of the chances of resolving social issues in American politics, and it is the impact of social or political crisis on this sense of the possible that gives crisis periods much of their distinctive character. Generally, crises are favorable for innovative approaches.

Normally cautious politicians suspend their resistance to untried approaches in view of the perceived necessity to respond promptly to the crisis. When any delayed response is guaranteed to fail, the adoption of uncertain expedients may suddenly become feasible.

Yet crises are not always the best occasions for producing good public policy. To begin with, the normal biases and delays in the policy process may be eminently sensible if they require the careful forging of consensus through reasoned consideration of the issue and its possible resolutions. Some actions taken in the heat of crisis probably should not have been taken, and *would* not have been taken except for the urgency of the moment. Charles O. Jones, in his study of national air pollution policy,[1] identifies a crisis period of "speculative augmentation" beginning in 1970. During this period, action outran knowledge and policy proposals escalated toward stronger regulatory control through the competitive efforts of politicians eager to get public credit for a strong stand on pollution. The normal political limits on major change were set aside, at least for a time, and politicians pursued a lopsided course of policy development.

The unusual level of political support forthcoming in most crisis periods has another problematic consequence, that of the impermanence of crisis solutions. The transition from crisis to normality is sometimes fatal for actions taken during crisis periods, and it is just this fact that provides the clearest evidence of the unusual political character of the crisis. The difficulty is that the change of attitude that often accompanies a return to normality may strike down effective solutions as well as ineffective ones. The second-thinkers who withdraw their support for a crisis-generated solution do so not because they have genuinely altered their judgment about the desirability of the solution in question, but because they have resurrected their precrisis prejudices. The crisis solution is "not something we would normally do" regardless of its record of success.

For example, the stringent controls on individual energy use

---

[1] Charles O. Jones, "Speculative Augmentation in Federal Air Pollution Policy-Making," *Journal of Politics,* **36** (1974), pp. 438–64.

in effect at the height of the 1973–74 energy crisis would not, for the most part, be acceptable public policy outside the context of that crisis. With the exception of the national maximum speed limit, whose continuation was eventually justified on the basis of evidence of proved gains in safety, not energy efficiency, direct personal restrictions on energy use were lifted as soon as possible. Some of the 1970 air pollution policy innovations were also retracted when political circumstances changed.

The final problem with crises as instruments of policy change is that they are usually in themselves dangerous and unpleasant periods that may be sources of further unresolvable issues and problems. The relative ease with which political resources can be mobilized in a crisis does not in any way guarantee that solutions can actually be found for problems unresolvable under normal circumstances. Policy makers will often be sufficiently busy dealing with the problems generated by the crisis itself that they will not seek out older problems stuck somewhere in the normal policy apparatus.

Consider, for example, the reaction of environmental groups and advocates of zero growth to the energy crisis of 1973. These groups were disappointed because the immediate response of policy makers was to weather the crisis, by reducing demand and rationing supply, rather than initiating long-term inquiries into life style changes and other approaches for coping with permanent shortage. In fact, because the hardships of the energy crisis had not been voluntarily incurred, the American public rejected out of hand any approach that seemed to call for continuing deprivation. Thus there was no good time to bring long-range energy policy questions before the American public, even though the need to do so had been dramatized by an energy crisis that could easily be repeated with similar effects if no action was taken to avert it. When the sun was shining, there was no need to fix the leaky roof; when it was raining, we were too busy trying to keep dry to take any constructive action.

Building Routine Responses

The examples of public problems cited in this chapter and the previous one, whether they are responded to or not, follow an "epidemic" model in which political demands are assumed to be only short-term disturbances in the political process. In this view, policy outputs succeed when the output of policy cancels the input of demands, so that a new social equilibrium is reached. Between demands, the political process returns to a normal state of quiescence to await the next demands. Failure occurs if no policy response emerges soon enough, or if the response does not cancel the input of demands. But in the epidemic model there is often only one chance for response; failure to cancel the input of demands may add to social unrest or add to cynicism about politics, but the demands themselves are assumed to disappear relatively rapidly whether they are effectively canceled or not.

Of course the political process is not normally quiescent. It may be so with respect to any particular issue, but since so many issues come up for resolution each year, the political process is rarely completely quiet. Thus timeliness is important in the epidemic model, and the time required for response may be significant in evaluating the process. Yet there are many issues for which an "endemic" assumption seems more realistic, and for which the element of time is largely irrelevant to the success of a policy response.

Endemic issue areas are those in which government policy is already implicated and governments therefore share partial responsibility for the current state of affairs. Issues, when they occur in these areas, often take the form of a questioning of the adequacy of existing government policy. Manipulation of the economy, social security programs, public services such as education, and even farm price supports are all accepted as permanent government tasks, although in each case these policies are built around substantial private initiatives in the same policy areas.

Issues in the areas just cited fall into the endemic category because they probably cannot be resolved unless governmental agencies assume some continuing role of regulation, subsidization, taxation and spending, and the like. There is also the danger, however, that issues susceptible to once-and-for-all resolution may instead become embroiled in unnecessarily routinized or institutionalized responses, and never be resolved satisfactorily. To see how this might happen, we must examine the political dynamics of routinized responses.

In contrast with crisis, periods of normality often bring the *political* opportunity to create a routinized response—that is, a pattern of regularized, almost ritualized debate about the issue, followed by negotiated incremental changes in the policies designed as resolutions for the issue. Incremental adjustments are the order of the day, for instance, when a policy is associated with a substantial budget, which must be refunded each year. Agency budget officers, usually in implicit collusion with legislative appropriations committees, identify and seek to protect the policy's budgetary "base," and to discuss changes only in the increment to be added to the base each year.[2]

The budget is the most strongly incremental policy-setting device yet invented, but it is not the only one. Any policy that fits easily into a simple policy evaluation mold, based on the more-or-less objective measurement of program effects according to discrete, quantifiable standards, may be treated in an incremental fashion. Target prices for farm commodities must be adjusted upward to keep pace with cost increases, for instance. Benefit levels in transfer payment programs such as Supplemental Security Income (the federally funded version of what used to be aid to the blind, aid to the permanently and totally disabled, and old age assistance), Social Security, and veterans benefits must likewise be pegged to living cost increases. Statutory minimum wage levels also require upward adjustment to the extent that the labor market will allow it. All these examples, except minimum wage laws, do translate into budgetary cost, but the primary criterion for adjusting the policy is the target, benefit, or guarantee level itself, not its estimated budgetary impact.

The adoption of an incremental, routinized approach offers advantages for nearly all political actors concerned with a particular issue. The burden of decision for nearly everyone is greatly reduced. Policy need not be rethought each time there is

[2] Aaron Wildavsky, *The Politics of the Budgetary Process,* Second Edition, Boston, Little, Brown and Company, 1974, pp. 102–23.

a need for adjustment because it rarely seems far enough wrong to be changed wholesale. Instead, some effects of the current policy—typically a guarantee level of some kind—have become marginally unsatisfactory. The effective political demand in these circumstances is likely to be one for service improvements rather than new policies; the demand is likely to come from an established group (and to be countered by other established groups); and the time pressure for response will be largely nonexistent. In most endemic issue areas, groups are active almost continuously, seeking marginal and remedial adjustments to policy and not new policies or major policy changes, and they are accustomed to achieving some measure of success, albeit incremental. Because the process is continuous it is virtually timeless, and policy adjustment proceeds largely according to its own internal dynamic.

The visibility of these issues is low because they rarely generate any "news" of sufficient interest to be picked up by news media. The word "opportunity" applies here as it does in the epidemic model, however, because the achievement of such an ordered pattern reduces the expenditure of political resources on an issue, lowers the uncertainty about the outcome for all participants, and guarantees some change and some measure of success for all interested parties.[3] Issues that can be shunted aside in this way can be resolved, in effect, even if debate about them continues periodically, because their routinization removes them from the public eye and releases the energies of interest groups and politicians to work on other issues.

Federal minimum wage legislation illustrates some of the features of routinized issue responses, and also shows the possibility that a formerly routinized response can be brought back into the realm of partisan conflict under the right circumstances. From its inception in 1938 until 1972, the minimum wage law (the Fair Labor Standards Act) followed a pattern of periodic change with great regularity and relatively minor political controversy. Typically, an increase in the basic minimum wage level, an extension

[3] Charles E. Lindblom, *The Intelligence of Democracy,* New York, The Free Press, 1965, pp. 213–7.

of coverage to previously excluded workers, or both, would be proposed in the first session of a Congress and passed in the second, just before the elections. This was the case in 1937–38, 1949–50, and 1965–66. In addition, the Democrats in Congress made an election issue of minimum wages in 1960, and passed an increase in 1961. An isolated rate adjustment occurred in 1955.

The congressional debates over minimum wage increases also followed the same pattern from one time to the next. The Department of Labor, Democratic congressmen, and representatives of organized labor would testify in favor of minimum wage legislation, and produce figures showing that the wage rate needed upward adjustment to keep pace with inflation and with wage rates elsewhere in the economy. Business representatives usually testified that they favored minimum wage laws, but that there was no current need to increase the wage rates, and to do so would cause inflation. The business groups would argue against expansion of coverage of minimum wage laws, producing statistics to show the adverse effects of coverage expansion on employment levels in the newly covered industries. Republican congressmen would complain that the constitutional assignment of regulatory power over intrastate commerce to the states was being undermined by federal encroachment. Union economists would attempt to counter all these arguments with their own statistics, and the Democratic majority on the committee would report a bill calling for needed upward adjustment in the minimum wage rate and, usually, coverage expansion also. Typically, the bill would increase the minimum wage rate gradually, in several steps, over a period of two or three years, and two or three years after the final increase had been made, a new set of increases would begin.

The last increase passed under a Democratic administration went into effect in 1967, and its mandated increases were completed at the beginning of 1971. Proposals for further increases were introduced in 1971, and the House and Senate passed differing bills in 1972, but strong business pressures prevented the compromise necessary to pass either version. A new set of proposals made in 1973 was acted upon by Congress, but it became a major partisan battleground when President Nixon vetoed the bill and Congress narrowly failed to override the veto. Giving in finally in 1974 to continuing inflation, and fearing that a second veto would be overridden, President Nixon signed a package of wage rate increases and coverage extensions very similar to those he vetoed in 1973.

Two factors combined in 1972 and 1973 to elevate minimum wage policy temporarily from its routine track into a major controversy. The built-in partisan conflict between Nixon and Congress showed itself on this issue as it had on others. In addition, the imposition of wage and price controls in 1971 delayed what might have been the routine increase in minimum wage rates, while at the same time committing President Nixon to take a stronger stand on any changes with probable inflationary effects than he might otherwise have done. With a Democratic president, and with a reduction in (or acceptance of) high levels of price inflation, minimum wage increases may again become routine.[4]

Putting Them Off Politely

Two other types of response to endemic issues, "oblique" and "standing," deserve mention because they are important in assessing how successfully the American political process responds to public issues of this type. What may be called an "oblique" response is simply an extreme form of a purely political routine response—a response not to the issue itself, but to the fact of organized groups and issue publics pressing one position or another on the issue. The intent of such a response is to mollify these groups, either by killing the whole issue or by putting them off with something less than they originally requested. The customary technique is co-optation.

The reason for an oblique response is not hard to find—it occurs when there is an abundance of political capital relative to the more tangible resources of money, expertise, and bureauc-

---

[4] An increase in the minimum wage was passed with relatively little controversy in 1977.

racy that would have to be charged against the general public if a real response were offered. Obliqueness is a politician's response strategy, since the gap between the issue broker or politician's desire to cater to client groups, and the impossibility of committing public resources for the direct benefit of the client group, is being filled by the politician's political capital.

Oblique responses differ from nonresponses because they occur under different circumstances. Nonresponses come from the epidemic model, with its implication of a single identifiable instance where response either happens or it doesn't; oblique responses assume an endemic situation. Because they feel the need to remain on good terms with the groups who must somehow be detuned from their original demands, politicians respond obliquely by co-opting the most vocal or powerful groups into the policy decision process, so that they will no longer be able to criticize policy makers from the outside.

Advisory panels, such as science advisors, often seem to be given this role. Presidents, especially, have been noted in the past for bringing important interest group leaders to the White House for well-publicized informal talks, obliging the group leaders, out of ordinary politeness, to temper any critical comments they might have made. President Johnson's commissions and task forces sometimes had this purpose. Republican presidents have worked in similar fashion with the Business Council, and President Ford's economic summit meetings had something of the same flavor. In short, it may be taken for granted that a political figure "holding court" or seeking to explain why things must be a certain way, is also seeking to co-opt potential critics and lay potential issues to rest before they can be joined seriously.

In a standing response, the response process may be described as "elevating an issue to a status." The approach is to acknowledge the existence of issue publics, to accept the legitimacy of their complaints, to extend sympathy and promises of remedial action, and then to take just enough action that the issue publics may see progress, but not so much that significant strides are ever made. To be successful, a standing response must confer a valued status at minimum cost to politicians and the public without insulting the recipients.

Standing responses probably do not occur intentionally. Tokenism is dangerous politics because the patronized groups may perceive that they could be getting more than they are. It would be difficult for a would-be tokenizer to know in advance what level of response is consistent with the limited availability of real responses and yet acceptable to the clientele group. The community action program, adopted as a major strategy in the War on Poverty in 1964, reveals some of the problems politicians encounter when they skate on the thin ice of tokenism. CAP programs created direct and tangible benefits for a few ghetto people, namely the community organizers financed by the program. Unfortunately for the larger client group, inner city residents generally, community organizers developed a vested interest in poverty—that is, in somebody else being poor. This perverse (though understandable) result, together with low funding levels for real projects, slow bureaucratic progress on those projects that did get underway, and growing local government opposition to CAP programs, led to increasing disillusionment on the part of inner city residents. To them it may easily have seemed that the government was not intending to alleviate poverty, but merely to identify and patronize it as a new social status.[5]

Politicians may blunder into a standing response, as they did with CAP, because the response choices for endemic issues are inherently limited. This can happen, for instance, if policy makers' intentions are to respond in an incremental fashion and they find nothing but status rewards to offer. Something like this happened to the working poor as the result of disagreements between Congress and President Nixon over the Family Assistance Plan. The working poor had been identified as the target for new income assistance legislation in the first FAP plan put forward by the Nixon administration in 1969. Between 1969 and 1972, when Congress finally gave up its search for consensus on FAP, the working poor had been talked about, measured, and experimented on, in an effort to design an income support program for them that would satisfy the objections of the working

[5] Theodore Lowi, "The Public Philosophy: Interest-Group Liberalism," *American Political Science Review,* **61** (1967), p. 18.

nonpoor. When FAP fell through and Congress in its place imposed stricter "workfare" requirements on existing welfare clients, the working poor emerged only with the consolation that their ranks had been swelled and they had been given a new status.

If politicians intend to make an oblique response, and the co-opted groups value the status conferred on them by this process, then again the result may be a standing response. In extreme cases, the original issue may be displaced entirely if the status rewards involved are sufficiently desirable that they, not the original issue, become the focus of new conflict. Recent consumer agency proposals have some of this element, especially if they should be passed with substantially diminished real powers.

If it is the case that a real response to a particular issue cannot be made, is it so bad if politicians respond in the only way they can, with some form of symbolic or co-optive gesture? Is this a response failure or not? The question is especially hard to answer when the client groups indulged by this process like what they get. Unless we are willing to impose our own standards, and say that they should not be happy because we, in similar circumstances, would not be, the only argument that can be made against symbolic responses is that they tend to prejudice the possibility of real responses immediately and for the future as well. The final chapter offers some suggestions for avoiding this fate.

9

Improving the Response to Social Issues

The main arguments of this book have been phrased in analytic language, and not the language of action. For example, interest groups *do* attempt to put issues on the public agenda, and they *do* worry about symbolic and "standing" responses, but not usually in those terms. So the main purpose of this concluding chapter is to translate the earlier analytic arguments into a strategic language.

Does the Process Need Improving?

Why should we coach social groups on conflict-raising techniques? Is there need for more citizen input? Government, it may be thought, should be a matter for experts. A great many political questions are dealt with every year, policies altered or confirmed, programs started and occasionally terminated, and personnel selected for important positions of public responsibility, with only minimal public scrutiny. There are at least two reasons why this arrangement is not satisfactory; one based on democratic theory and one on the realities of political organization.

It is the peculiar bias of democratic theory that there is a public interest in all operations of government and that it can be determined only by open public discussion. In this view, the

165

public interest is served best by the discussion of public issues because the actions most effective in bringing about governmental response are usually also the most effective for broadening and informing the public debate on the issues of the day.

These beliefs have been given concrete expression in recent years in the "sunshine bills" and freedom of information laws passed by many states and some local governments. These reflect more than just a suspicion that "something is going on" in the bureaucracy that must be watched closely; they also express the positive sentiment that what is "going on" is public business, at every stage of the decision process. Bureaucrats' sometimes indignant, sometimes dismayed defense that they really are trying to serve the public welfare too, or that there are important security reasons for withholding information, is increasingly regarded with suspicion. Bureaucratic unwillingness to open office doors and files, even though it means great inconvenience, disruption, and expense for government agencies, is "proof" that there is good reason for duplicity and concealment—evidence of improper influence, personal scandal, or just plain bungling and incompetence.

Bureaucracies are easy targets these days, and it is not the intention here to imply that bureaucratic footdragging *is* necessarily evidence of malfeasance. Most of the responsibilities given to American bureaucracies require voluntary cooperation from the regulated interests if they are to be successful. The glare of publicity, in the name of the citizen's right to know, often dries up this voluntary cooperation, whether the agency has anything to hide or not. So unless we are willing to grant a firmer hand to our government bureaucracies to allow them to act effectively on their own initiative, there are limits to the further extension of openness within the government apparatus itself. Happily there are no such limits at the initial stages of issue controversy. Instead, there are practical reasons to *encourage* involvement, regardless of our assumptions about the nature of the public interest.

The oldest models of popular, participatory democracy assumed that all questions were public questions. To the extent that there was disagreement in such a system, every question would become a public issue. At the same time, the older models often assumed a large degree of community of interest within the governing unit—the local community or the classical city state. Thus there would be earnest public discussion of many questions, but often the discussion would result in substantial agreement on the appropriate course of action. Indeed, open discussion among all citizens of the polis was valuable in itself, because it was the best way to discover a basis for agreement.[1]

Most people would say that we no longer live in a polis. In pluralist democratic theories, any question could still become a public issue, but only on the basis of conflicting private or individual interests, rather than individual participation in a communal interest. Furthermore, individuals are assumed to be concerned only about the few questions that affect them directly, so that plural interests find expression as plural issue concerns. Rarely will the entire citizenry be found to be concerned with the same issue. Resolution furthers the pursuit of individual interests, and produces a moment-to-moment "traffic-director's order" rather than achieving any higher, shared, purposes.

Here, in the pluralist world, the ability of all groups to lobby for their own concerns is especially important if the results of the issue translation process are to avoid economic and class bias. In the pluralist approach, social issues often rise to prominence as pleas for government intervention on behalf of some underprivileged group, and resolution of these issues is popularly regarded as a decision in favor of the underprivileged claimants. Theirs are the sort of claims that do not enjoy automatic access to political power, and that must force a political response to be successful, so at worst the encouragement of issue-raisers merely balances the well-known status quo biases of American politics. In any event, a public issue strategy is not a closed device. Anyone can use it. Advice on the effective exploitation of social issues may be taken up more rapidly by some groups than others, but this bias comes from the near-exclusive reliance of

[1] Traditional arguments along these lines are reviewed in S. I. Benn and R. S. Peters, *The Principles of Political Thought,* New York, Collier Books, 1964, Chapter 15, and A. D. Lindsay, *The Modern Democratic State,* New York, Oxford University Press, 1962.

those groups on public appeals, not from the unavailability of this approach to others.

How to Define an Issue: Opportunities

The subject of this book has been governmental responsiveness. A sensible strategy to achieve greater responsiveness must tie into the basic parameters of governmental action discussed in Chapters 2 and 3: governmental (or social) knowledge, governmental (or social) capacity, and political (or public) will. The word "social," or "public" has been added to each of these three parameters to suggest that they are not immutable: appropriate strategies can change any of these toward greater responsiveness to a particular social issue. At any stage, the general strategy is simple:

1. Make up for the lack of governmental knowledge.
2. Improve governmental capacity.
3. Hope for and encourage the exercise of political will by individual politicians.

To apply this analysis to the problem of defining an issue, the best approach is to make use of every opportunity to generate an issue that presents itself. For example, seizing upon a political crisis, or even precipitating one, may be useful for some groups. In some ways, a group's behavior is cynical if it deliberately foments a political crisis—it is not directly seeking a resolution of the issue, and it is consciously exploiting latent disagreements in a strategy that may not be the best for resolving the issue conflict once the issue is raised. The cynicism inherent in a deliberate escalation of social conflict is, however, partially balanced by the dangers of the strategy; that is, crisis response is almost certainly less predictable than the results of a carefully engineered compromise. Black power advocates, for instance, and practitioners of confrontation politics in the 1960s realized the limitations of a deliberately provocative approach, but they adopted it, with all its limits, as the only effective strategy open to them. It was, at least for those groups with serious issue concerns, an action of desperation and disgust rather than cynicism.[2]

[2] Stokely Carmichael and Charles V. Hamilton, *Black Power,* New York, Vintage Books, 1967.

Standing government policies or continuing programs also provide ways of generating issues. They can perform this function by introducing new, formalized processes for deciding on the specific applications of general policies. The most pervasive use of this approach can be found in the regulatory field, where permits are required to erect certain kinds of building, dump certain kinds of waste, carry out certain kinds of land development, sell certain kinds of products, or mine certain mineral resources. Typically, the general policy statement governing issuance of such permits is exceedingly vague. Where permits are required, at some time in the past a legislature responded to a social issue by creating a policy to regulate, but it delegated the specific task of regulatory standard-making to a regulatory agency or commission. To protect itself against charges of having given away legislative power, the legislature concerned (city council, state legislature, or Congress) usually provided for a public hearings stage prior to the final ruling, and also for judicial appeal from unfavorable judgments reached by the regulatory agency.

The effect of both these procedures, the public hearings and right of judical review, has usually been to provide an opportunity for alert citizens or organized interest groups to force a more careful and balanced consideration of the case at hand than would otherwise have taken place. The procedures for preparing and evaluating the environmental impact statements (EIS) required by the National Environmental Policy Act, and parallel state laws, are another such arrangement. An informed citizen or interest group, if it is vigilant, can use the draft environmental impact statement as a lever to force more open hearings and discussion of a pending project before the final decision to issue a permit is made.

In most instances, the procedures are relatively detailed and also reasonably fair to potential opposition, spelling out such matters as how long in advance of a decision a potentially controversial application must be published, how it must be published, the nature of the evidence to be considered, procedures for hearings, and so on. By themselves, however, these arrangements will not generate an issue, any more than they will by themselves dictate that the viewpoint represented by the larger group of citizens will win out. Instead, they are programmed opportunities. They place certain constraints on the regulators, but they also assume that objectors are capable of certain things. They insist that regulators pay attention to reasoned or numerically significant opposition, but at the same time they assume that such opposition will come forward of its own accord, and will do so at a time when a permit application has perhaps not yet become controversial. The only thing automatic about the whole procedure is the automatic availability of an opportunity to be heard; if this is passed up for lack of knowledge, lack of organization, or lack of an effective proponent for the other viewpoint, then the opportunity will have been lost.

Achieving an effective response may prove particularly difficult in policy areas dominated by a well-established subgovernment, yet the strategies here are the same as in other areas where subgovernments are not as firmly entrenched. Ripley and Franklin identify three general approaches, all dependent ultimately on subgovernments' potential internal weaknesses.[3] There is hope for change (1) if the subgovernment disintegrates of its own accord, as the sugar lobby did in 1974; (2) if Congress or high-level executive officials step in and exert their formal oversight and budget powers, as happens from time to time with the regulatory agencies; or (3) if a subgovernment takes on new jurisdictional authority that generates internal tensions before subgovernment members can readjust themselves, as may have happened to some of the agencies involved with energy matters. In all such cases the lesson for outside groups is simple: be prepared to take advantage of any break in the subgovernment's defenses. Seize opportunities for change whenever they occur.

How to Define an Issue: Solutions

The development of several social issues discussed in this book suggests that the form in which an issue is debated can be highly significant, both for its reception in governmental circles and its eventual chances for resolution. Unfortunately, there is little an

[3] Randall B. Ripley and Grace A. Franklin, *Congress, the Bureaucracy, and Public Policy,* Homewood, Ill., The Dorsey Press, 1976, pp. 6–7.

individual group can do to control issue definitions, since they change in the course of public discussion and are often, themselves, a product of compromise among conflicting issue publics. The urge may be, mistakenly, to seek the clearest definition of the issue at the earliest stage.

It is not usually serious that public goals are not "clarified" by processes of public debate, or even by official responses to public concern, since a priori clarity of goals is largely irrelevant to subsequent government processing. With the exception of those seeking purely symbolic rewards, there is no advantage in premature clarity. The real action-relevant question is, "what changes can we get?," meaning "what changes are politically achievable?" The answer to this question emerges from group interaction with governmental decision makers and cannot be predicted in advance of the decision; hence a premature fixing on one specific demand may often be an inappropriate strategy because its fixity may hamper necessary compromise. Why seek clarity without an input of governmental realism?

In short, the basic process might be more usefully described as "publicizing" an issue rather than "defining" one, and in this respect it leads naturally into the next stage, expanding the claimant public. Publics are reached by publicizing, and a sensible definition strategy looks forward to likely groups to be added to the emerging claimant public. Cobb and Elder, building upon Schattschneider, suggest that issues can be expanded most effectively (1) by keeping their definitions ambiguous, (2) by arguing that they have wide and enduring social significance, (3) by portraying them as simple questions that demand immediate response.[4] Rephrasing this advice in the terms used in Chapter 4 to describe the public agenda, we can say that the ideal issue definition should combine the elements of opportunity and public worry. If this can be done, the largest possible audience will be mobilized. Specific issues in the consumer field, such as food safety, have certainly been expanded in this fashion.

Where can a public be found, socially, geographically, and

[4] Roger W. Cobb and Charles D. Elder, *Participation in American Politics: The Dynamics of Agenda Building*, Boston, Allyn and Bacon, Inc., 1972, pp. 112–23.

institutionally? The image of the interest group executive, operating on a shoestring budget from a cramped office and soliciting financial support from the membership lists of other established organizations, is just one of the traditional ways this essential part of the process may be carried out. Public relations stunts designed for mass media coverage may also work to raise the public profile of a group, but then individual citizens must seek out and volunteer their support for the group. When local environmental groups make their "Dirty Dozen" awards to state legislators with the worst environmental records, they are hoping to stir up trouble among the constituents of those legislators and at the same time attract additional contributors to support the group's work.

Although the assumption that governments will "naturally" respond to any significant social problem has been shown to be simplistic, it may often be helpful for a budding interest group to conceive of its organizational problem as "making up for" a lack of governmentally sanctioned knowledge about social problems and their solution. This is true because a politician's main interest is to find a problem *for which there is a solution ready to hand.* Political will is bound up with the availability of tenable positions, meaning (at a minimum) solutions as well as problems. If problems have been suppressed for want of a solution, perhaps they can be brought into the open again by publicizing a solution. If the temper of the times is right (and this is beyond the control of individual groups anyway), good solutions may almost "call forth" problems from the list of perennial worries every society has.

An illustration of this approach, although an unsuccessful one, can be found in the activities of the Citizens' Committee for Children of New York. This long-standing organization, formed of concerned doctors, academics, politicians, family and juvenile court judges, and civic leaders, became interested in the idea of children's allowances through the work of one of its research committees. The Committee, with financial assistance from the Ford Foundation, sponsored a conference on the subject, with nationwide participation, in 1967, just as national discussion of welfare reform alternatives was beginning. Conference participants then took the message back to their local organizations around the country, and some of them subsequently sponsored local conferences to explore the utility of children's allowances as a contribution to overall reform of the welfare system.

The significance of this illustration is the fact that it began with a solution not a problem, and that its action focus was only vaguely political. The thrust of the Citizens' Committee effort was to inform a national child welfare "elite" about the operation of children's allowances in other countries, and perhaps to persuade them that the device could work in the United States. Beyond that, the members of this loosely defined elite group would have to carry the discussion forward within their own organizations and localities. Childrens' allowances did not catch on, and within two years of the national conference the Nixon administration had taken the initiative by proposing the Family Assistance Plan, but the initial organizing efforts of the Citizens' Committee did contribute substantially to the social discussion of welfare reform.

How to Build an Effective Organization

The step from issue definition (however vague or definite) to mobilization of an issue public requires organizational resources. What, exactly, are these resources, and where can they be found? They are numbers, money, and status; these may be turned into persuasive power and into political access. All other supposed assets fall under one of these headings.

NUMBERS
Sheer numbers of supporters must always be recruited, and a group's issue position is an important basis for attracting support. But rarely does the mere existence of an unorganized group automatically call forth supporters. Members must be recruited by direct advertising, indirect publicity about the group and its activities, raiding the membership lists of similar groups, adopting or co-opting the membership of another group wholesale, and so on. All of this inevitably means a great deal of monotonous work with low payoff, locating address lists, solicit-

ing memberships by telephone or letter, and keeping detailed records (as may be required for tax purposes).

What good are numbers? Basically, numbers are a measure of credibility. The perennial question asked of interest groups, in tacit or overt form, is "and how many people do you represent?" The centrality of numbers (= votes) to political calculus places a premium on sheer organizational size, and the significance of a political argument may be seen, for good or ill, through the lens of organizational strength (for which size is the handiest surrogate). Numbers *do* translate into votes, but only when a group takes an unequivocal stand on individual politicians, and then only to the extent that group members follow the cues from this one group to the exclusion of others (organized or unorganized) to which they also belong. Still, these conditions are found occasionally. The Dirty Dozen awards made by environmental groups nationally and in various states show the potential of numbers, especially when other organizational resources are lacking. Legislators rightly fear being put on the Dirty Dozen list because they know that large numbers of people, members of the citing organizations and chance members of the general public, will hear about the "awards" and act on them at election time.

MONEY
Numbers also translate into money, and money is a source of security for organized interest groups because it rents headquarters space and equipment, purchases supplies, pays workers, and perhaps even allows some leftover for further organizational efforts. Money is also security in the form of a professional "finish" to group activities—a sense that the group must be reckoned with because it knows its business and will be around for some time to come.

STATUS
Status refers to the ability of a group to penetrate the network of protective defenses surrounding official policy makers, and thereby to insist on being heard and responded to. The interest

group leader's most important asset is access, and access can usually be achieved only by persistent effort over a period of time. Interest group representatives must prove themselves knowledgeable and reliable, because politicians want to protect their scarce time against useless inputs. Thus there is a "grandfather clause" governing the acquisition of status.

In some fundamental ways, status and access are synonymous, but the two make distinct contributions to the expansion of issue publics. Access itself provides only a source of authoritative information for an issue entrepreneur; social groups will respond to such information only if they believe it to be accurate (and they have no sure way of knowing that). Status, being basically reputational, may be achieved without direct reference to questions of public policy. It must, at the same time, be cultivated by group leaders—*actual status* must be sought among politicians, and the *reputation for status* must be reinforced among group members. When all this is done successfully, group leaders enjoy an expanding clientele and the clientele enjoys substantial access in the right governmental circles. Organized groups with the reputation for being "in the know" will control the field, and push out lesser interest groups. They, and not the others, will be looked to for evidence of policy changes and opportunities.

The point is that groups active over the long run should take the achievement of some status in politics as a major goal. By the nature of things, status can be achieved only with regard to endemic issues—public problems that extend over a period of years and generate incremental solutions. Allowing oneself to be co-opted by a government bureaucracy is one way to achieve status; another way is by catering to an individual dissident politician whose actions are newsworthy. In this latter instance, the legislator's notoriety contributes to news media coverage, and media coverage in turn contributes to publicity for the group viewpoint.

In the realm of endemic issues an interest group need not always go looking for support among government bureaucrats. Some government agencies seek to maintain a loyal and active clientele, especially those agencies whose initial policy successes were credited to active public support. Thus in the air pollution control field, national air pollution control agencies encouraged direct citizen involvement from the beginning of air pollution control programs in the middle 1960s. As citizen frustrations grew and became clearer, the agency relied on them to pressure Congress to add stronger enforcement powers and to refine regulatory standards. The state and defense departments, to name just two of the most venerable executive agencies, also have large and well-known outside supporters that they cultivate by a variety of methods.[5]

The "big time" in expanded issue publics is represented by Common Cause, Public Citizen (the Ralph Nader organization), and a few other omnibus public interest groups. These loosely structured organizations have attempted to institutionalize an issue public through expanded membership rolls and appeals to the supposed common sympathies of the members. They can gain about as much free publicity as they want from carefully timed press releases pointing out new dangers, lamenting a decline in standards of quality or safety, or criticizing a governmental agency. A mix of local and national orientations is prominent in both Common Cause and the Nader establishment. Public Citizen, for instance, includes under its umbrella Congress Watch, litigation, regulatory oversight, local citizen action, and local public interest research groups. The statewide PIRG's are especially effective devices for creating large, diffuse issue publics by recruiting college students to work on matters of local concern.

Student activism had its heyday in the 1960s, but perennial academic idealism can still be invoked from time to time to mobilize an issue public. In a recent instance, the NAACP, through the National Student Coalition Against Racism, organized the 1976 National Freedom March on Boston to show sympathy with the locally controversial school busing program there. With the rallying cry "the attacks in Boston are attacks on us," groups organized in many cities to travel to Boston or to help finance the march. The chosen date, May 17, was

[5] Francis E. Rourke, *Bureaucracy, Politics, and Public Policy,* Boston, Little, Brown and Company, 1969, p. 17.

symbolic—the anniversary of the 1954 *Brown v. Board of Education of Topeka* decision—and the march was largely symbolic as well. It is hard to imagine the local opponents of busing being anything other than outraged to see thousands of outsiders descending on an already tense situation. Yet as a strategy to mobilize a frustrated national issue public, the Boston march was probably as effective as anything else that could have been done.

One final illustration may underline the occasional significance of the element of chance in mobilizing support. The area of tax reform is a perennial governmental issue. Politicians often claim a desire to reform the tax laws, and every significant change in the tax code is hailed as "tax reform," especially if it reduces someone's tax burden. By and large, the public seems inured to these protestations of good faith from politicians because, in fact, the tax laws do not change very much for the average taxpayer. So the tax reform issue would not seem like a fruitful area for mass public involvement. Yet something in the nature of a "taxpayers' revolt" occurred in 1968 and 1969, and it gave rise to some significant tax law changes as well.

In 1968, Joseph Barr, an Undersecretary of the Treasury, began publicizing new Treasury data, based on a large sample of tax returns, showing the actual federal tax burden at various income levels.[6] The data, he said, showed an unacceptably high level of variability in actual tax rates paid because of special tax treatment of certain kinds of income such as investments and tax shelters, the deductibility of interest and charitable contributions, and so on, and he called for immediate tax reform to close some of these loopholes.

The mass media were not overly impressed by the matter of effective tax rates, but they were attracted by the existence of several hundred millionaires who, legally, paid no income tax at all. These figures were splashed around widely, and an embarrassed Congress—where the tax laws making all this possible had been written—rushed to respond by proposing the imposition of a token 10% "minimum income tax" on anyone who had other-

---

[6] See, for example, Joseph W. Barr, "Tax Reform: The Time Is Now," *Saturday Review,* March 22, 1969.

wise succeeded in avoiding tax liability. This plan, along with a number of lesser changes, was enacted in 1969.

Why did Barr's campaign against tax loopholes "succeed" when others before it had not? Four factors seem to be critical. First, the facts spoke for themselves, and they presented the reform argument much more clearly than had been done before. Second, Barr continued his campaign through 1969 (after he had left office) until it achieved success, thus contributing his authoritative voice to the momentum for reform. Third, others were writing the same things, so that public attention was concentrated in this one area—a welcome relief, perhaps, from the rigors of Vietnam. Fourth, it did manage to spark media attention and a surprisingly high level of interest among the general public.

But these four reasons do not really explain why Barr's campaign succeeded. Reason 4, especially, says little more than that Barr's proposals succeeded because they succeeded. What *does* explain the success of the 1968–69 taxpayers' revolt, although it is less palatable to would-be social issue advocates, is that somehow the time was right for such a proposal. Barr's efforts were essential, but the fact that they were followed up at each subsequent point, where they might instead have dropped into insignificance, shows the equally essential presence of other factors. For a recurring issue like tax reform, the best advice to offer to issue publics is to be prepared to push hard for an issue when the circumstances do seem to be favorable. In the meantime, small scale efforts to raise the same issues may help to monitor their changing social acceptability and help to "soften up" the public against the time when an all-out effort can be successful.

How to Play to Your Strengths

For any interest group setting out to redress a grievance nationwide in scope, whatever the level of resources it may enjoy, the objective chances of success must be daunting. The problem is only slightly better than that faced by the isolated voter who says, "what difference does it make if I vote or not—my one vote won't count for anything." Just as it does little good to dredge up the historical examples where one vote *did* make a difference, so it is useless to assure an interest group blithely that "every little bit helps," when it is already convinced that "every little bit goes for nought," and only big bits will make any headway against entrenched political interests and institutionalized biases.

There is a best strategy to follow to conquer the "immensity problem." Put simply, it is to work in a small enough arena that occasional success can be virtually certain. The American system of federal sharing of responsibilities among levels creates real opportunities to raise and resolve national social issues at state and even local levels. This is true not just of specialized, local issues, but of nearly every kind of social issue. The key is to realize the limited role played by any single interest group, no matter how well organized and supplied with resources, in the overall process of issue translation, and to build upon these more realistic expectations.

How does this work? There is, first of all, the much greater ease of building an issue public and an organization at the local level than at higher—hence larger—levels. Local interest may focus initially on "bread and butter" concerns such as schools, parks, liquor licenses, police patrols, traffic lights, and property taxes. Temporary revulsion with national politics seems to spur a renewed sense of local political community in many cities, indicated by a revival of interest in community newspapers, neighborhood associations, cooperatives, civic betterment projects, and the like. The community development block grants provided by the federal government since 1974 support this movement indirectly by requiring representative citizens' advisory committees. The fledgling politicians hatched in this exercise of grass roots democracy—under the stimulus of federal grant-in-aid money—have remained active, many of them, in local volunteer politics.

Further, local public agencies seek to encourage—or is it try to co-opt?—citizen advisory bodies. Groups formed originally for citizen input on school policies, or the disposition of special revenue sharing funds, have been recruited as sources of advice by public services such as bus systems. Public Citizen, Common Cause, and other nationally based citizens lobbies have sought to encourage all locally organized forms of direct democracy, and they have contributed substantial sums and organizational effort to form local groups and tackle important local problems. These lobbies, as well as nearly every other organized Washington interest group, are federal in form. Their organizational strategy is simple:

1. Individual members affiliate with state or local branches of the parent organization.
2. Members work in the local branch on matters of local importance, and develop organizational loyalty to the local branch.
3. Meanwhile, members' contributions support the national organization, its nationwide organizing effort, and its Washington lobbying.

Many of the issues cited in this book sit uneasily at the federal level. The appeal to Washington (to Congress, or to the Supreme Court) is often an effort by disgruntled groups at state or local levels to go over the heads of local politicians. Abortion, most matters of educational policy, law enforcement, questions of morality, and nearly all laws relating to the use and transfer of property and the licensing and regulating of economic enterprise, are state prerogatives. In turn, most of the overt public issues in these policy areas come to the fore as purely local matters—offenses against public order or community standards that arouse definite public reactions based on clearly perceived common interests.

Difficulties in local enforcement of air and water pollution control laws, and resulting citizen discontent, contributed directly to strengthened national legislation in these areas. The abortion and death penalty issues are still essentially state questions. Local opponents of school busing can hardly say that they have been ignored in the making of national policy. It is precisely their opposition that has led to national delays, vacillation on the part of presidents, attorneys general and Supreme Court judges, and Congressional attempts to blunt the local implementation of court rulings. In none of these areas could the local viewpoint have been so formidably expressed if local citizen groups had not been active.

Formally or informally, many national issues are in fact resolved by adding up the impact of local political forces. On most questions passing through Congress, members are not allowed to forget that they represent local constituencies. On an important partisan political issue such as aid to education, for instance, the "peak association" sends word to its members to crank up the pressure machine, and the member organizations in turn send word to their state and local affiliates. The affiliates then mobilize their members to apply pressure to their home state representatives. Here the effectiveness of local political organization is manifest.

Consider these further illustrations of local political power:

1. When majorities of both parties in Congress unite to override a presidential spending veto, even though the president has attempted to make the veto a partisan matter, the nature of the spending program usually shows that members of congress are responding directly to local sentiment.

2. When the National Federation of Business and Professional Women's Clubs (the peak association for the Equal Rights Amendment) announces a ratification plan for ERA—drawn up for them by a well-known firm of political consultants and concentrating on a list of target states—it is clear that many national policies are made by the 50 states acting collectively.[7] The consultant's plan goes on to identify "inside" and "outside" strategies for each state, in each case directly dependent on effective local and grass roots lobbying efforts.

3. Finally, when the National Wildlife Federation submits an environmental priorities ballot to its members, asking them to return their responses *and* their state of residence, this organization is obviously trying to assess its support base and also prepare to lobby from different viewpoints in each state.

[7] "Consultant Firm Plans Rights Passage Strategy," *Minneapolis Tribune,* December 13, 1974. See also Kay Mills, "ERAmerica Coalition Gearing Up for 15-State Fight for Ratification," *Minneapolis Star,* September 21, 1977.

In most respects, state political institutions are patterned after those at the national level, but a few states are wide open politically to citizen initiatives. Efforts to recall Mayor Rizzo of Philadelphia and Mayor Cavanagh of Detroit, among others, and the successful recall of the Detroit school board over integration plans,[8] suggest the dangers of miscalculation on the part of local politicians. California has been notable for many years for its citizens' energetic use of their initiative powers. Recent attempts to legislate directly on the complicated matters of nuclear power plant siting and the "right to die" forced the hand of state government, and legislation was passed in these areas under strong influence from citizen lobbies.

As an expression of citizen sentiment, the initiative device is invaluable, but as an instrument of legislation it must be used with some care. For instance, a 1968 California initiative against open housing passed overwhelmingly, but it was subsequently overturned by the state Supreme Court. The lack of adequate citizen organization, or the lack of a tradition of citizen initiative, is probably a more serious barrier than the courts in most states. The legacy of Populism and Progressive reform sentiment totals 22 states with initiative provisions, 25 with a referendum, and 14 states with a recall; yet few of these states make much use of these devices.[9] The citizens' lobby in California reportedly can mobilize 10,000 volunteers to canvass for signatures (at least 325,000 are needed) on an initiative petition.[10] California is a large state: even 10,000 *signatures* in many another state would go a long way toward meeting the legal requirement for an initiative, referendum, or recall, yet these provisions often lie dormant. Here, certainly, is a significant and nearly unexploited means of raising and resolving social issues at the state level.

Robert Weissberg's careful review of the evidence on direct democracy supports this view, but it also emphasizes the limits on the effective use of initiative, referendum, and recall proce-

---

[8] William R. Grant, "Community Control vs. School Integration—The Case of Detroit," *The Public Interest*, **24** (Summer 1971), pp. 62–79.

[9] Ralph Nader, "Enlarging Self-Government," *Minneapolis Tribune*, November 23, 1974.

[10] Ralph Nader, "Enlarging Self-Government."

dures.[11] Overall, the courts have been at least as supportive of direct legislation as they have of enactments of state legislatures. The content of direct legislation is no more sweeping or radical than legislative output of the same time period. Finally, the public does not stampede to approve initiatives—this route is less successful than legislative proposals submitted to public referendum.

Ultimately, direct legislative procedures must reflect the attitudes of those clever enough to make use of them. In North Dakota, for example, Robert McCarney has almost singlehandedly nullified $200 million of state spending plans since 1963 by adroit use of the state's referendum provisions.[12] Weissberg's estimate of $1 million for an initiative campaign does not apply here: a mere 7000 signatures will force a referendum in North Dakota. Once the issue is on the ballot, state residents understandably vote against raising their own taxes. Certainly direct legislation can be used for positive purposes too, but the bias of public politics often runs the other way. The successful fight for California's Proposition 13, which mandated an immediate 57% rollback of property taxes, illustrates this point perfectly. The initiative itself gives local officials absolutely no guidance on how they should cut their budgets by the $7 billion annually the initiative requires.

How to Get a Real Response

We come, finally, to the most problematic part of the whole translation process: the payoff. Recall the discussion in Chapter 2 of issue resolution. What is, after all, a real response? It seems to depend on how patient we are, how dramatic we insist the response should be, and most importantly, whether we insist also that an honest governmental response resolve the issue at hand. This question is shot through with so many ambiguities that it

---

[11] Robert Weissberg, *Public Opinion and Popular Government,* Englewood Cliffs, N.J., Prentice-Hall, Inc., 1976, pp. 67–72.

[12] *Time,* June 13, 1977, p. 19.

may be more useful to ask instead "how can we keep politicians from ducking the issue?"

In many ways, the answer to this question is implied in the foregoing sections of this chapter. The basic strategy is to encourage the exercise of political will by politicians, and the easiest way to do this is to show them how their political self-interest coincides with a favorable response to a particular social issue. With the "politician as bloodhound," searching out just such issues and giving them active encouragement, this is not a difficult task. With the "politician as reluctant St. George" (the more normal type), more patience, more organization, and more careful cultivation of political access will usually be necessary. When politicians enjoy entrenched positions—judges with life tenure, legislators from safe seats, executives moving up to another level of government—citizen activists may have good reason to be discouraged.

Much of the success enjoyed by issue publics in the examples cited in earlier chapters is either conditional or situational; conditional on the availability of solutions, and situational in that successful responses are more often forthcoming in "fat years" and periods of crisis than in "lean years" and stretches of dreary political normality. If there is a key to success in the raising and resolving of social issues, it must take into account these uncontrollable external influences on the issue translation process, and it must suggest ways for issue publics to survive the relative dry spells they will inevitably encounter.

One key to success is a counterpart to the doctrine of modest expectations presented in Chapter 2. There, modest expectations of governmental effectiveness were counseled; here, modest expectations for the effectiveness of political activism are in order. Governments are the most inclusive political organizations in their respective jurisdictions; to force politicians in governmental positions to act against their bureaucratic judgment or self-interest may require a counterorganization of almost equal size. Short of a mass citizenry bent on revolution, there is little chance of building such an organization. It will be undermined, co-opted, or defused in some other way before it becomes a serious threat to politicians trying to hold onto their positions of institutional power.

How, then, can the doctrine of modest expectations be put to any positive use? How can it be advocated without undermining the idealism, sense of commitment, even radicalism that form the basis for sustained individual political interest? First, issue publics must be prepared to spend much of their time "playing the game"; that is, they must participate in the political routines and patterns of incremental policy adjustment associated with "endemic" and routinized social issues in the United States. If, and this is a big if, groups can maintain some independence while participating in these processes, they will be prepared to take advantage of the occasional opportunities for major change by which some few issues are resolved from time to time. These opportunities are not the norm, they are the exception. Yet they are not ultimately separable from the routine processes of issue translation, and issue publics disdaining participation in those routines will be ill-prepared to recognize or take advantage of breaks in the routine.

Where, for instance, would the pro-abortion and pro-life factions be now if they had not been looking over the shoulders of state courts and state legislatures through the many years of desultory action on the abortion question? What would be the chances of ratifying the Equal Rights Amendment if women's rights groups had not built a groundwork within each state, organized, raised (male) legislators' consciousness of women's rights questions, and elected (male and female) legislators sympathetic to their cause? In retrospect, the opportunity to achieve any kind of environmental protection commitment—before the energy crisis hit—was so short that groups initially organized by the environmentalism movement of the late 1960s would not have had enough time to achieve anything substantial before their opportunity passed. They swelled the ranks, but would there have been any ranks to swell if conservation groups and ecologists had not been at work long before the popular rise of environmental concern?

The development of national policy on pornography and gun

control further reveals the advantages of being organized and being there first. There is no pornography lobby, and the gun control forces have come into the contest too late to overcome the initial advantages of the gun lobby. The possibility that these issues may persist is the only hope for groups not now favored by public policy in these areas, for they will probably have no effect until they have organized and fought for access alongside the groups supporting the status quo.

How, finally, can issue publics avoid the dangers of co-optation? How can they avoid "losing the faith" when circumstances are not favorable for their point of view? Happily, the answer to these questions is beyond any theorizing or advice-giving of the sort attempted in this book. Groups lose faith if their members lose faith; groups are renewed by the continuing renewal of membership. Social issues cease to be social issues if their issue publics fall away, but continuing recruitment of new members may sustain issue publics *as long as the issues themselves are matters of concern to individual citizens.* Ultimately, there is no other motivating power for the issue translation process, or for political life of any sort.

To Read More

My method in writing this book has been largely empirical, drawing examples from newspaper and magazine reports, secondary sources, and personal observation, but rarely from the scholarly literature. Nevertheless there are some works in the social sciences I have found particularly useful, and I will cite them here because they are much easier to find than the diverse collection of examples I have used to illustrate the text.

Robert A. Dentler has a valuable discussion of the concept of "social problem" in *Major American Social Problems* (Chicago: Rand McNally, 1967). Social conflicts and their dynamic elements are discussed in Lewis A. Coser, *The Functions of Social Conflict* (Glencoe, Ill. The Free Press, 1956), and E. E. Schattschneider, *The Semisovereign People* (New York: Holt, Rinehart and Winston, 1960). Two additional works are useful sources on interest group organization: Mancur Olson, Jr., *The Logic of Collective Action* (Cambridge: Harvard University Press, 1965), and Theodore J. Lowi, *The Politics of Disorder* (New York: Basic Books, 1971).

A number of recent books provide comprehensive analytic treatments of the policy process. Charles O. Jones, *An Introduction to the Study of Public Policy* (Belmont, Calif.: Wadsworth Publishing Company, 1970), is the most systematic treatment of this subject. Roger W. Cobb and Charles D. Elder, *Participation in American Politics: The Dynamics of Agenda Building* (Boston: Allyn and Bacon, 1972) emphasizes the processes for the identification

187

of social and governmental action commitments. Ira Shar-
konsky, in *The Routines of Politics* (New York: Van Nostrand
Reinhold, 1970), suggests the pervasive role played by regularized procedures and policies. Two works explore systemati-
cally the close connection between types of public policies and
the nature of the political forces that grow up around them.
These are Theodore J. Lowi, "Four Systems of Policy, Politics,
and Choice," *Public Administration Review*, **32** (July–August,
1972); and Randall B. Ripley and Grace A. Franklin, *Congress,
the Bureaucracy, and Public Policy* (Homewood, Ill.: Dorsey Press,
1976). Odom Fanning, *Man and His Environment: Citizen Action*
(New York: Harper and Row, 1975) presents an optimistic assessment of the possibilities of citizen activism, especially at the
local level. Government policies and national public opinion
polls are compared in a number of policy areas in Robert
Weissberg, *Public Opinion and Popular Government* (Englewood
Cliffs, N.J.: Prentice-Hall, 1976).

A great deal has been written recently on social indicators and
program evaluation techniques. Good general introductions are
Raymond A. Bauer, ed., *Social Indicators* (Cambridge: MIT
Press, 1966): and Carol H. Weiss, *Evaluation Research* (Englewood Cliffs, N.J.: Prentice-Hall, 1972). The Brookings Institution recently published books on two major social policy
experiments that introduce the method of social experimentation and reveal some of its pitfalls. These are Edward N. Gramlich and Patricia P. Koshel, *Educational Performance Contracting*
(Washington: Brookings, 1975), and Joseph A. Pechman and P.
Michael Timpane, eds., *Work Incentives and Income Guarantees*
(Washington: Brookings, 1975).

Policy case studies tend to be ephemeral. I have found these
useful, among others: Eugene Eidenberg and Roy D. Morey, *An
Act of Congress* (New York: Norton, 1969); Kenneth M. Dolbeare
and Phillip E. Hammond, *The School Prayer Decisions* (Chicago:
University of Chicago Press, 1971); Michael P. Smith and as-
sociates, *Politics in America: Studies in Policy Analysis* (New York:
Random House, 1974); Robert L. Peabody, ed., *Cases in American
Politics* (New York: Praeger, 1976); and David A. Caputo, ed.,
The Politics of Policy Making in America (San Francisco: W.H.

Freeman and Company, 1977). Paul Sabatier's article "Social Movements and Regulatory Agencies," *Policy Sciences,* **6** (Fall, 1975) provides a model that could be emulated with profit, building more general theoretical conclusions from case studies in the area of air pollution.

Index